zamzam of spiritual knowledge

Zamzam of Spiritual Knowledge

Shaykh Mohamed Faouzi al-Karkari
may Allah sanctify his secret

Translated by Marouen Jedoui
Compiled by Mohamed Jedoui
Edited by Ouiam al-Karkari

⌐⌐ LES 7 LECTURES

A CELESTIAL ORGANIZATION
BUILT ON EARTH
AL·KARKARI
INSTITUTE
BY SHAYKH MOHAMED FAOUZI AL-KARKARI

أعوذ بالله من الشيطان الرجيم

بسم الله الرحمن الرحيم

بسم الله الرحمن الرحيم

بسم الله الرحمن الرحيم

بسم الله

بسم الله

بسم الله

الله

الله

الله

ولا حول ولا قوة إلا بالله العلي العظيم

Table of Contents

Translator's Preface 17

Introduction 21

Session I 25

The Disciple Has Found the Door to Happiness 25

The Intensity of Divine Light: A Sign of Proximity 27

Certainty and Intention Are the Keys to Every Prayer 28

The Illness of Laziness 29

Learning to Say *al-Ḥamdu Lillāh* 30

Vision in a State of Wakefulness: *Mushāhada* 31

How Does a Disciple Ascend to the Heavens? 31

Da'wa Among Disciples of Opposite Sex

Is Strictly Forbidden 32

What Is the *Subḥa*? 33

Praying for One's Head of State 33

Do not Be Veiled by the Modesty of the Shaykh 35

Session II 37

The Difference Between Illusion (*khayāl*)

and Vision (*mushāhada*) 37

The Karkarī Disciple and Marital Obligations 39

It Is only Through Heedlessness That One Does

not Send Blessings upon the Prophet 41

The Peril of Forsaking One's *Wird* 42

How to Cure Hypocrisy 45

When You Come to the *Walī*, You Embark

on a Migration Towards Allah 47

Session III 51

Swimming in the Two Seas: The Sea of *Sharīʿa*
and the Sea of *Ḥaqīqa* 51

Separation (*faṣl*): Bridging *Sharīʿa* and *Ḥaqīqa* 53

The Enlightened by Allah and the Astray in Philosophy 54

The Love of Allah 57

Session IV 61

The Prophet's Central Role in the *Lām* 61

How Can a Disciple Become the Shadow of the Shaykh?....63

The Staves of the Shaykh: A *Lām* and an *Alif* 66

The Light of Believers and the Words of Hypocrites.....67

The Trial of Doubt: The Road to Hypocrisy....................69

The Misguidance of Neo-Sufis...70

Session V 73

The Perfection of Ādam's Vessel....................................73

What Is "the Clay Resonant as Pottery"? 75

The Earth as a Reflection of Humanity:
The *Maghrib* as its Heart...77

The *Siyāḥa* in the Body: Multiple Points of Entry,
the Heart as the Sole Point of Arrival 78

Session VI 83

Optimizing One's Visit to the *Zāwiya*............................83

The Importance of the Group in Monitoring the *Nafs*....87

Prostrate to Him, and the Mountains Will Follow 88

The Love for the Shaykh Is More Important
Than the Vision of the Light..89

The True Enemies of the Shaykh 91

Everything Originates from the Shaykh 92

Beware of Asking Allah for the Station of a *Walī* 93

Beware of Falling into Incarnation (*ḥulūl*)
and Unity (*ittiḥād*) 95
The Birth of a Daughter Is Always Good News 96

Session VII..**99**
Understanding the Nature of Light Is a Good Sign........99
Always Return to the Source 100
The Manifestation of the *Qabḍa Nūrāniyya*
(Luminous Grasp) Illustrated by the Earth....................100
Changing Destiny? 101
All Answers for the Believers' Questions
Are Found in the Word of Allah..............................102
What Is *Jalāl*, Truly? 103
What Is the Difference Between a Prophet,
a Messenger, and a *Walī*? 104
The Confrontation Between *Risāla* and *Wilāya*
in the Story of al-Khiḍr and Mūsā............................105

Session VIII **111**
This World Is Merely Ruins, Therefore
Do not Attach Yourself to It 111
The Star Is Light: The *Nafs* Is Darkness 112
The Lower World (*dunyā*) Is a Defilement..................113
Allah's Light Is Everywhere with the Disciple,
but the Disciple Is not Always with Allah 114
Accepting Things as They Are 115
Learning to Converse with the Lord..........................116
Permission for *Siyāḥa* Is Mandatory,
as Is Starting it in a Group 117
The Patched Garment Reflects the Lamp 118
How to Visualize the Light?..118

Trials as a Sign of Divine Love................................119
The *Qibla* in the Maghreb...................................120
Patched Clothing: The *Sanad* (evidence) of 'Umar.......121
The only Authentic *Khulwa* Today.........................122
Sanad of the *Subḥa* in the Qur'ān.......................122
The Shaykh Will not Instruct a Disciple to Adhere
to the Foundations of the Path; This Responsibility
Falls on the Disciple Himself.................................123
Shame Befalls One who Asks the Prophet
to Purify His Heart...124
Denounce Yourself Before Becoming the Mockery of All...125
Focus on Your *Nafs*..127
The *Mīm* Studies the Heart Through the Colors
of the Forty Stations of the *Nafs*..........................128
The Shaykh as the Hundredth Name 130
Session IX 131
Everything That Veils You from the Light Originates
from Your *Nafs*...131
Tasting the Divine Essence Through the Attribute 132
Contemplating a Single Formula to Know Him.............132
Meditation Through *Dhikr* Transmitted by the *Wāsiṭa*.....133
The *Wāsiṭa* as Either a Veil or a Gateway 134
Begin Meditating on the Heavens Before the Earth.......135
Why Does Man Desire Wealth and Worldly Goods? 136
How to Escape Earthly Attraction? 137
Surpassing the Seven Heavens to Understand Earth.....138
Reading the Qur'ān in the Heavens for Understanding 140
How to Ascend Through the Heavens?.......................141

The Only One to Achieve Total Knowledge
of His *Nafs* Is Our Prophet Muhammad 143
Elevation Through the Heart, Not the Intellect.............144
The Door to the Light Is Unique: Islam,
While All Other Doors Originate from the Dajjāl..........146
Al-Khalīfa al-Maknūn (The Hidden Viceregent)...........148
Who Will Be Saved in this Journey to Allah?....................150
What Is the Solution for Allah's Servants to Be Protected?..152
Followers of Falsehood and People of Truth....................154

Session X 157
Henna, a *Sunna* of the Prophet....................................157
Disciples as the Shaykh's Children 158
The Esoteric Significance of Palm Lines on both Hands...159
Implementing What Is Understood to Reach the Secret...160
The Disciple and the Universe..160
Ultimately, Your Efforts Stem Solely
from the Grace of Allah..161
The Two Major Levels of Commitment to Allah............162
Giving Charity to the Shaykh?...163
Preaching the Light of Allah Is the *Sunna*
of the Prophets and Messengers.......................................164
The Lamp, the Example Leading to Truth.......................165
The Dots...166
The Language of the Secret: the Line and the Dot.........167
Understanding the Qur'ān: Returning
to the Embryonic State..169
One Should Never Alter the *Wird* Taken
at the Commitment with the Shaykh...............................170

The Knowledge of Allah Can only Be Transmitted
Through Piety, Which Is a Light................................172
Waken when Others Sleep 173
Session XI... 175
Erasing Prior Knowledge to Welcome the Light.............175
What Did the Shuyūkh Do to Their Disciples
in the Past to Achieve this Foundation?.......................176
The Intellect and the Spiritual Journey......................177
Emptying Oneself of the Understandings Acquired
Before the Path of the Three Stations of Islam 178
Reflection (*tafakkur*) Is Dependent on Continuous *Dhikr*....180
How Did the Prophet Receive His Knowledge?.............183
Journeying through Colors..184
Primary Colors and Their Shadows 185
The Body Is Directed by the Heart 186
What Does the Heart That Conceals All Secrets
Represents, the One That Is in True *Tawḥīd*?...................187
Who Can Truly Understand *Tawḥīd*:
The Unique Position of *Ahl al-Bayt* 188
Indeed, He Who only Thinks
of the Perishable Is Perishable 190
Why Must One Who Seeks the Truth
Go Through Sayyidunā 'Alī?.....................................191
What Does Sayyida Fāṭima Represent? 192
Lām 194
The Core of Religion: *Lām* and *Bā'* (*lubb*)..................195
Who Is Connected to the *'Itra* of the Prophet?.............196
The *Lām*, a Rope That Extends from Heaven to Earth 198
Qubb 198

The *Lām*: The Vital Connection Between *Lā* and *Mīm*....200

Session XII **203**

The Disciple's Obligation to Fulfill
the First Reading 203

The Heart That Contained Him 206

The Notion of Centrality...209

How Did Mūsā Reach Realization?...........................212

Why Did Allah Name Him Shuʿayb?.........................213

Do not Be Like the *Aʿrāb* (bedouins)......................215

Daʿwa that Becomes an Obstacle to *Dhikr* Is Invalid.....216

Hārūn: The Interpreter of Truth...............................217

Gentleness in *Daʿwa* in the Face of Tyranny 217

Session XIII **219**

Dreaming of a Swamp, a Stream, or Similar....................219

Following the Light by Clinging to Its Source 220

Meditation Must Be Accompanied by *Dhikr* 222

How Does Allah Purify Our *Nafs* from Its Vices? 225

Enduring Trials on the Path of Allah............................226

Everything That Comes from the Sea Is Pure 227

Completing the Manifestation of an Incomplete
Name Through *Dhikr* and Following the *Sunna* 228

Love in *al-Qabḍ*..229

How to Love Seclusion..230

When Allah Responds to Our Prayers 231

The Love of the Righteous Leads to the *Walī*................232

Everything Begins with a Flash....................................233

Everything Prostrates 233

Session XIV August 18, 2021 .... **235**

The Use of Charity and *Zakāt* Funds in the *Zāwiya* 235

Translator's Preface

In the Name of Allah,
the Most Merciful, the Very Merciful.

All praise is due to Allah ﷻ, Lord of all worlds, Who has guided us to the path of righteousness and granted us the light of faith. We glorify Him with words that fall short of His majesty, and we exalt Him with hearts that are humbled by His infinite mercy and wisdom. Peace and blessings be upon the Seal of the Prophets, our master Muḥammad, the Mercy to all creation, who conveyed the Message with clarity and grace, and whose light illuminates the hearts of the faithful until the Day of Judgment.

May the choicest blessings and most abundant peace be upon his noble family and his righteous companions, who carried forth his luminous legacy with sincerity and devotion. And may Allah sanctify the secret of our Shaykh, the radiant guide and beacon of truth, Sidi Mohamed Faouzi Al-Karkari, *Quddisa Sirruh*. Through his blessed presence, may the veils of heedlessness be lifted from our hearts, and may we be granted the ability to perceive the Divine Reality with the eye of certainty.

By the grace of Allah ﷻ and under the luminous guidance of my Shaykh, I humbly present this work, seeking the pleasure of the Almighty and the intercession of His Beloved, the Prophet Muḥammad, as well as his inheritors from the elite of his blessed family, may peace and blessings be upon them all. May this effort serve as a source of benefit and light for all who seek the path of truth.

Realizing that translation into English is a key gateway to spreading the path of Allah ﷻ to the farthest horizons, and encouraged by the positive reception of my previous translation of Sidi Shaykh's teachings, *Candles on the Path*, I embarked in December 2023 on a new translation project. This time, I focused on the book that my brother, Sidi Mohamed Jedoui, compiled in the summer of 2023: *Zamzam al-Maʿrifa*. This book contains valuable teachings from the Shaykh, imparted during the early stages of the revelation of the second reading of the Name "Allah," the *lām of contraction and passion*. I quickly realized that translating this book would help fill a gap in our literature, as it addresses crucial aspects of wayfaring (*sulūk*) on the path that are scarcely covered in other books written during the *hā'* phase. This book is a valuable resource for both newcomers and seasoned disciples, written in a simple language that touches on the essentials of *sulūk* and *maʿrifa* needed to apprehend the *lām* of the singular Name.

I translated the book over two periods: during the winter break of 2023/2024 and the summer of 2024. I based this translation on the French version, which was easier to work with. Since the person who compiled the Arabic text is the same one who translated it into French, I trusted that the original meaning had not been altered. I would like to thank my brother, Mohamed Jedoui, for helping clarify his writings when things became a little confusing. I also extend my gratitude to Lella Ouiam AlKarkari for her assistance with editing; without her contribution, this book would not have seen the light of day. I am grateful to my parents, Dr. Anouar Jedoui and Dr. Essia El Ouadi, and my brother, Khaled Jedoui, for their unwavering support throughout this process. I also thank my sister, Dorra, for recording sections of the book and making them available to English-speaking disciples on the Tariqa's YouTube page. Finally, and most importantly, I thank my Shaykh for his blessings. Without his spiritual support and permission, this book would not have come to fruition. I am honored that he has used me for this task, and I pray that Allah Almighty continues to use me as a vehicle for spreading his light and wisdom.

We ask Allah Almighty for ease, prosperity, and a blessed ending on our path. Āmīn!

Marouen Jedoui
New Haven
Yale University

Introduction

In the Name of Allah, the Most Merciful, the Exceedingly Compassionate, He who transcends the states of non-being and the attributes of diminution. Blessings and Peace be upon Our Prophet Muḥammad, the Quintessence of the Secret, the Fountain of Love, and the Sage of the Science of Monotheism, as well as upon his family. Through the blessings of Shaykh Sidi Mohamed Faouzi Al-Karkari (author of this *basmala* and prayer upon the Prophet), may Allah sanctify his secret.

During more than two years of devoted service at *Zāwiya Karkariya*, Sidi Shaykh, may Allah sanctify his secret, bestowed upon us the permission (*idhn*) to translate into French the teachings he imparted nearly every day after the ʿasr prayer, and on Fridays following the *ḥaḍra*. We broadcasted these teachings live on social media for the benefit of French-speaking disciples. By his grace, this became an almost daily practice.

One day, Sidi Shaykh, may Allah sanctify his secret, signaled to us that we had amassed sufficient lessons and it was time to consolidate and transcribe them. Henceforth, we explored methods to transcribe the teachings, continuing our translations to ensure French-speaking disciples continued access to Sidi Shaykh's teachings.

In a conversation about *Zāwiya's* matters, Sidi Saïd Zinnid—may Allah protect him—observed that many disciples had ample time to transcribe Sidi Shaykh's sessions. He suggested that in a subsequent phase, other disciples could refine and finalize this transcription effort.

This was a sign and directive from Sidi Shaykh guiding us in the compilation of these translations. Consequently, we embarked on finding disciples willing to transcribe our translations, aiming to create a robust database, with the long-term goal of compiling these teachings into a book.

Responding to this call, a group of female disciples stepped forward: Lalla Sarha Berrehail, Lalla Camélia Mekki, Lalla Malika-Sara Merzoug, and Lalla Rachida Kaddouri. For over two years, they diligently transcribed many teachings, including those in this book. Notably, the translation of a single teaching could extend beyond an hour and a half, making the transcription process quite arduous. This group also played a crucial role in editing and validating the teachings. Other disciples, including Sidi Abdelqader Benoit, Lalla Essia El Oued, Lalla Sona Ouedraogo, and Lalla Nawal Séverine—may Allah preserve them—contributed to the transcription and editing work.

This book presents a selection of Sidi Shaykh's full teachings from the period immediately following the Tariqa's delving into the first secret of the *lām* of passion, after over thirteen years in the study of *hā'* of identity. It offers responses to a diverse array of inquiries, guiding seekers in this stage of their spiritual journey. We endeavored to maintain utmost authenticity, striving for a translation that is both accessible and resonant, in straightforward, relatable language for our readers.

In conclusion, we extend our heartfelt gratitude to Sidi Shaykh for entrusting this noble task to us. We pray to Allah—the Almighty—for His protection over Him, His blessed family, and all His beloved. We also thank all disciples who devoted their time and energy to this project, a pursuit we deem the most significant of our lives. Our gratitude extends to our parents, siblings, for their unwavering love and support. We beseech Allah, through Sidi Shaykh, to let this project be a beacon of Light, interceding on behalf of our families, ancestors, descendants, fellow disciples, and all those who have contributed, near and far, to its fruition.

Mohamed El Jedoui

Session I
September 16, 2020

*

The Disciple Has Found the Door to Happiness

The Light within our hearts is the source of all the Lord's beauty ﷻ. All that is noble is Light: the five pillars of Islam are Light, the Qur'ān is Light, and the Prophets are Light.

Whether it is the Name or the Attribute, Light always returns to the Essence, which is Allah ﷻ. Those who doubt the vision of the Light inadvertently affirm that Light is darkness, which implies that Islam is darkness and that Allah ﷻ is darkness. This is indeed the path that Shayṭān (Satan) has chosen for the unfortunate. If the disciple does not strive to rid himself of these satanic thoughts, he will in turn become a *shayṭān*, may Allah ﷻ protect us from this.

This Light is described in the Qur'ān. In *Sūra* al-Nūr, verse 35, Allah ﷻ says: **Allah is the Light of the heavens and the earth. The exemplification of His light is like a niche within which is a lamp, The lamp is within glass,** the glass as if it were a resplendent star, Lit from [the oil of] a blessed olive tree, Neither of the east nor of the west, Whose oil would almost glow even if untouched by fire. Light upon light. Allah guides to His light whom He wills. And Allah presents examples for the people, and Allah is Knowing of all things.

Allah ﷻ has definitively encapsulated these four examples within this Qur'ānic verse. The perception of the Light remains true to this hallowed framework. Consequently, introducing any additional examples beyond the aforementioned four constitutes, in itself, a deviation into disbelief. The revelation of this Light ought to fill us with joy, as Allah ﷻ (Glorious and Majestic) has graciously unveiled the eye of our heart, enabling us to witness this verse in its true essence.

The *walī* (saint) thus raises his disciple from the station of *al-islām*, where the Muslim simply recognizes the existence of the Light, to the station of *al-īmān*, where the believer witnesses this blessed Light. This remarkable transition, confined to a remarkably select group and pivotal to the entire teachings of *wilāya* (sainthood), should fill the disciples with profound happiness, as we are assured that Allah ﷻ has guided us away from misguidance. The issue, however, is that the disciple often lacks the mental and spiritual awakening necessary to fully appreciate this joy, as he does not revere what he perceives.

Through this divine blessing, all Karkaris have surpassed the boundaries set by exoteric sciences. It is essential to recognize that even the least knowledgeable among the Karkarī disciples holds a level of certainty and understanding that the most erudite exoteric scholars have yet to attain.

*

The Intensity of Divine Light: A Sign of Proximity

When Allah ﷻ described the Niche, He did not specify its size or proximity. If we were to describe it according to the Qur'ānic text, we find that the Niche resembles a ring, a setting in which there is a Lamp that can be likened to a jewel. This jewel, the Lamp, is protected by a Crystal. This ensemble, the Lamp and Crystal, takes the form of a celestial body. To measure the intensity of the Light in these examples, we must turn to the sunna of our Prophet ﷺ.

Abū Hurayra ﷺ narrates, as recorded in *Ṣaḥīḥ Muslim*, that the companions asked the Messenger of Allah ﷺ: "O Messenger of Allah! Will we see our Lord on the Day of Resurrection?" The Prophet ﷺ replied, "Do you have any difficulty in seeing the sun at midday when there are no clouds?" They said, "No." The Prophet ﷺ then said, "Do you have any difficulty in seeing the full moon when there are no clouds?" They said, "No." The Prophet ﷺ then declared, "I swear by Him in Whose Hand my soul is! You will not have difficulty in seeing your Lord just as you do not have difficulty in seeing them."

The intensity of the Light seen by the believer will then be measured by the two aforementioned examples: the moon and the sun. To these two, we add the vision of the brightest star in the sky. The more intense the Light, the greater the knowledge of Allah ﷻ, the more present the blessing, and the closer the disciple is to Allah. This proximity seals the answer to every prayer.

*

Certainty and Intention Are the Keys to Every Prayer

The disciple who is close to the Light is close to all the Names of Allah ﷻ, for all Names are Light. Take, for example, the Name *al-Shāfī*, meaning the Healer. If in his *istighfār* (seeking forgiveness), the disciple sets the intention to heal from a disease through the Light of this Name, he will be healed.

Some disciples may question why this doesn't happen for them, even though they witness the Light? There are two factors preventing the disciple from achieving his desires. The first is his lack of certainty in Allah's ﷻ response, and the second is his wavering, unsettled intention. For example, a disciple might begin his *wird* (litany) intending to heal from a disease, but then his *nafs* (ego) diverts him from this initial intention towards another. It might tell him that he instead desires to acquire knowledge.

Thus, the disciple remains astray, struggling to focus on a single intention. If the disciple wished to become wealthy, he could achieve it. He just needs to focus his *dhikr* (remembrance), illuminated by the four examples, on this intention. Indeed, he would activate the Name *al-Mughnī*, The Fulfiller of Needs.

At the same time, we can attribute anything to *istighfār*, and becoming wealthy isn't the only thing a disciple could attain. He could also perceive what is hidden in the *malakūt* (celestial realm), traverse time and space, and cure all ailments.

Know, O disciple, that this journey is of disconcerting ease, for your Shaykh has already prepared everything you need for successful travel. It is as if you were to travel without needing to obtain a passport or even a visa. Your Shaykh has taken care of everything; you only need to set an intention, which will be your destination, and he will lead you there.

*

The Illness of Laziness

A disciple told us about a blockage preventing him from performing his litanies, uncertain whether it stemmed from his nafs (self) or elsewhere.

The inability to perform one's *wird* is, in reality, nothing but laziness. The true ailment here is sloth, for one finds the energy and means to do other things, yet pretends to be hindered when it comes to fulfilling the commitment made to the Prophet ﷺ and his heir. Be aware that your *nafs* will not leave you in peace; it will exert all its strength to erect barriers between you and the Shaykh, between you and the disciples, and between you and *dhikr* (remembrance of God). Its desire is for you to indulge in laziness and vices. If you are on this path, it is for your purification, to elevate yourself on the path of Allah ﷻ, to distance you from bad habits, and thereby to know the Real. For this purpose, cultivate sincerity within yourself, cease attributing fault to others, and diligently endeavor towards earnestness and dedication in your spiritual path.

*

Learning to Say *al-Ḥamdu Lillāh*

Some seekers with a repugnant past lament their lack of Light. They sometimes say, "O Sidi Shaykh, we only see a dot of Light."

Should you not rejoice in having this immense mercy with you, proof that Allah ﷻ has forgiven your tainted past? To avoid arrogance, always remember who you were before joining the Tariqa.

*

Vision in a State of Wakefulness: *Mushāhada*

A disciple in the session claimed to have ascended to the heavens and seen the prophets after performing the wird. Sidi Shaykh reprimanded him for lying and defines mushāhada.

The vision received by the disciple from the Shaykh has clear conditions. First, the disciple sits to perform his *wird* or *dhikr*. At that moment, the Light appears in his vision. He is in a perfect state of wakefulness.

The best of visions is that of the Light because it is clearly mentioned in the Qur'ān; it is the core essence (*ḥaqīqa*) from which Allah ﷻ created everything. It appears through the four examples mentioned in the verse of Light. From this vision also emanates the visions of forms and images (*ṣuwar*).

*

How Does a Disciple Ascend to the Heavens?

This question is legitimate, as ascending to the heavens is not an ordinary occurrence. This ascent is made through the four examples of Light. These are the vehicles through which we can travel through the heavens and the earth. Furthermore, the heaven in question is never visualized in its totality. The Shaykh will in reality place the disciple at a point belonging to a well-defined heaven, and from that point, he will visualize what has been prescribed for him of the creation of that heaven. Sometimes, the disciple believes he is ascending to *al-muntahā* (the Farthest point or Lotus of the Limit) and sees himself entering an incredible source of Light; in reality, he is just trying to surpass the limit of a heaven.

*

Daʿwa Among Disciples of Opposite Sex Is Strictly Forbidden

Daʿwa among disciples of the opposite sex is strictly forbidden. This aligns with the teachings of the *sharīʿa*, which is the foundation upon which the seeker builds his path and is the first key to understanding the journey. Unrelated men and women cannot engage in *daʿwa* with each other. If a foreign woman asks a disciple about joining the Tariqa, he must provide her with the *wird*, inform her that she must perform it for 40 days, and then direct her to the sisters, and vice-versa for women. This is to prevent excesses and to ensure the disciple's flourishing on the path of Allah ﷻ.

*

What Is the *Subḥa*?

Sidi Shaykh discusses the subḥa (rosary) following a dream experienced by a disciple. In this dream, the disciple enters a mosque and finds many subḥas. He then approaches the imam of the mosque, who informs him about the dire state of the community and the trials endured by Muslims. Deeply moved, the disciple begins to weep.

The *subḥa* is a tool created by Muslims to facilitate the remembrance (*dhikr*) of Allah ﷻ. The real power of this object lies not in its matter of style, but in the number of illuminated *dhikrs* performed with it. The more a disciple uses the *subḥa* for *dhikr*, the more it becomes charged with Light.

*

Praying for One's Head of State

The Prophet ﷺ urges Muslims to take to heart the issues of the community, to be attentive, and to exhibit compassion towards one another. However, Muslims must not forget that the priority is to rid themselves of flaws and purify their *nufūs* (souls). Being aware of the community's problems does not mean blaming the apparent wrongdoers. The Sufi knows that the true fault lies within; all good comes from Allah ﷻ and all evil from our *nafs*. Anything negative in the journey originates from oneself. One must begin by addressing oneself, meaning we should heal the darkness within ourselves, including our eyes, hands, feet, ears, and so on. At the same time, it is important to pray for all Muslims and their leaders.

In the *Zāwiya*, many prayers are made for the leaders of Muslim states, as Allah ﷻ has chosen them to manage the affairs of Muslims. If a disciple understands what their role represents for the entire community, all their prayers would be directed towards them. Indeed, state leaders bear responsibility for all the *nufūs* (souls). Furthermore, in the sunna, the Prophet ﷺ encourages us to remain steadfast in our obedience to the leaders of the Muslim community.

Imam Muslim ؓ reports in his *Ṣaḥīḥ* that the Prophet ﷺ said: "The best of your rulers are those whom you love and who love you, who invoke God's blessings upon you and you invoke His blessings upon them. The worst of your rulers are those whom you hate and who hate you, and whom you curse and who curse you." It was asked, "Should we not overthrow them with the sword?" He replied, "No, as long as they establish prayers among you. If you find something detestable in them, you should dislike their actions, but do not withdraw from their obedience."

Imam al-Bukhārī ؓ reports in his *Ṣaḥīḥ*, on the authority of 'Abdullah ibn Mas'ūd ؓ, that the Prophet ﷺ said: "You will certainly see favoritism and things that you disapprove of after me." They asked, "What do you instruct us, O Messenger of Allah?" The Prophet ﷺ said, "Fulfill their rights and ask Allah for your rights."

We are honored to have a king as our head of state, as his title, "*al-malik*", is also one of the beautiful names of Allah ﷻ. Additionally, the King of Morocco is a descendant of the Prophet ﷺ and is reverently referred to as *amīr al-mu'minīn* (the Commander of the Faithful) by the Moroccan people.

If all Muslims made *du'ās* (supplications) for their head of state, they would be content, and their governors would be good and just. Today, many Muslims despise their governors, whereas they should pray for them. The Shaykh prays in *sujūd* (prostration) for the leaders of Muslim states. He also teaches his Muslim disciples in Europe to be grateful to the authorities of their countries, as they protect them and provide for their sustenance. As such, they should pray for Allah ﷻ to guide these authorities towards Islam. Some immigrants often complain about the authorities of their countries and even go as far as to insult them. It is better for them to return to their countries of origin if they feel such disdain.

*

Do not Be Veiled by the Modesty of the Shaykh

In the past, some disciples filmed the Shaykh during his private sessions, and then audaciously broadcast them on social networks and in groups hostile to the Tariqa.

The Shaykh prohibited the disciples from recording the sessions, concerned about their potential decline in decorum in future years. He was aware that some would exhibit behavior lacking in modesty and decorum.

Let anyone who thinks the Shaykh is weak and debilitated by his health know that they are completely veiled from the truth of the Shaykh. Whoever becomes an enemy of the Shaykh will be destroyed by Allah ﷻ.

Everything that happens today in the Tariqa was meant to unfold exactly in this way, for as soon as we entered into the *lām* of passion (*lām al-'ishq*), a filter was activated, automatically repelling the hypocrites.

Session II
October 16, 2020

*

The Difference Between Illusion (*khayāl*)
and Vision (*mushāhada*)

Illusion originates from the disciple's imagination, while vision arises in a state of wakefulness and does not belong to the realm of the imaginary. Vision arises from Allah and is perceived through the *baṣīra*, the eye of the heart. This form of seeing is religiously permissible and acknowledged by Islamic jurisprudence. In experiencing the vision of the Divine, one does not use the physical eyes or the *nafs* (self), but rather the spiritual, Divine sight. The legitimacy of such visions is corroborated in *Sūra* al-An'am, where the Real (*al-Ḥaqq*) reveals to Prophet Ibrahim ﷺ the *malakūt* (celestial realm) of the heavens and the earth. Those who harbor doubts (*was-wās*) about their visions, considering them mere figments of imagination, should recognize that such skepticism leads them astray from the path of Allah ﷻ.

Sayyidunā 'Alī ؓ proclaimed, "I am the dot." If a disciple perceives a point of Light, it signifies standing at the threshold of the Gate of the Real. Those who do not embrace this belief, who doubt that the Lord has the power to do as He wills with His servant and reveal to him as He pleases, should remove the *subḥa* (rosary) from around their neck and align themselves with the Wahhabis (implying that they are out of place both in the presence of Sidi Shaykh and within Sufism). Therefore, prior to commencing their spiritual journey towards Allah ﷻ, disciples are urged to perform the prayer of consultation. Should a disciple still harbor doubts about the Light being a divine manifestation, even after Allah ﷻ has shown signs that the Tariqa is a path leading the servant to Him, this reflects a profound ailment of the soul. Such individuals must introspect and reassess their understanding of Islam. In the realm of *al-īmān*, a Muslim is called upon to firmly believe in the unseen realms, encompassing entities like the angels, the prophets ﷺ, the concept of destiny, and the Day of Judgment, as ordained by Allah ﷻ.

*

The Karkarī Disciple and Marital Obligations

In a dream, a disciple sees Sidi Shaykh smiling. He had 27 white teeth and one black.

Understand that when someone dreams of the Prophet ﷺ or a *walī* (saint) with an imperfection, it should be seen as a reflection of himself. Indeed, the dream serves as his own mirror. For example, if in the dream, the disciple sees them in jeans or without a beard, it signifies that the dreamer has deviated from the sunna and needs to realign with it. Prophets, emissaries of Allah ﷻ, and *awliyā'* (saints) should appear in visions in their most exemplary postures, embodying the true essence of the sunna.

In the context of teeth symbolism, it's critical to recognize that Islam adheres to a lunar calendar comprising 28 lunar days, paralleling the 28 teeth depicted in the dream. Allah ﷻ communicates to this sister that she has faithfully observed her worship on 27 days, with the black tooth representing a day of neglected duties.

Teeth also symbolize family members: the front upper teeth, such as the incisors, which are visible and prominent, symbolize the immediate family members (father, mother, husband, brother, sister). In this instance, the blackened canine tooth indicates that either her husband or someone intimately close is resistant to the disciple's commitment to the Tariqa.

A Muslim woman embracing the Tariqa must exercise wisdom, as she is required to dedicate time to her *dhikr*, amounting to a maximum of 3 hours and 15 minutes daily: the two *wirds* (morning and evening) approximately take 90 minutes, daily Qur'ān reading around 45 minutes, and the night *dhikr* spans a whole hour. If her husband opposes her participation in the Tariqa, she should discreetly practice her *dhikr* and refrain from discussing the Tariqa in his presence.

Should a woman fail in her marital responsibilities, her husband's affection may diminish, even if the Prophet ﷺ personally bestowed the *wird* upon her. It's important to understand that the ideal wife is one who serves her husband, embodying his home and sanctuary as the Qur'ān suggests. Absence of this homely essence upon his return can lead to inevitable discord. On the other hand, if the woman's conduct aligns with the Qur'ānic teachings, it greatly increases the likelihood of Allah ﷻ guiding him towards the Tariqa.

In another dream, this disciple witnessed water flowing from her house and saw herself consuming honey.

The water's exit from the house symbolizes the removal of an affliction, as water purifies, a concept echoed in the Qur'ān. Consuming honey in the dream represents healing, aligning with the Qur'ānic revelation that honey serves as a remedy for people.

*

It Is only Through Heedlessness That One Does not Send Blessings upon the Prophet

An Egyptian disciple experienced a dream where every cell of his body was engaged in majestic and intense prayers for the Prophet ﷺ. Consequently, he sought Allah's aid in maintaining a continuous connection with the Prophet ﷺ.

Regardless of the individual's will or his religious beliefs, every human body sends prayers upon the Prophet ﷺ. This occurs irrespective of whether one is a Muslim, Catholic, Buddhist, Jew, Satanist, or atheist. His body is in a state of constant prayer upon al-Muṣṭafā ﷺ. As the Qur'ān declares, everything performs *tasbīḥ* (glorification) to express gratitude to Allah ﷻ. All existence is sustained by the Mercy of Allah ﷻ, and it is well acknowledged that this Mercy is personified in our beloved Prophet ﷺ. Hence, everything naturally prays upon Him ﷺ. Sent as a Mercy to all of humanity and the entire cosmos, the Prophet ﷺ is the source from which all existence derives. Should the cells of the human body cease their prayers upon the holy Prophet ﷺ they would vanish, as they owe their existence to his Mercy ﷺ.

When a disciple recites prayers upon the Prophet ﷺ he unites his entire being, awareness, and every limb in devotion to him; these acts are mere affirmations of what his body naturally does by Allah's will.

*

The Peril of Forsaking One's *Wird*

A female disciple sent a private message to Sidi Shaykh, expressing regret for having taken the bay'a (initiatory pledge) in June 2020 and subsequently neglecting her wird. She failed to perform it within the prescribed time and eventually ceased altogether, also discontinuing her attendance at Shaykh's sessions. She attributed this to doubts (waswās) about the Tariqa and lamented having squandered her life.

This act is tantamount to breaking the covenant. The essence of the *bay'a* (initiatory pledge) lies within the *tasbīḥ* (*wird*), which must never be abandoned. The Light of Allah ﷻ serves as a testimony against anyone who neglects his commitment. Moreover, listening to the Shaykh's teachings offers a taste of divine proximity.

It is critical to understand that neglecting one's *wird* represents a catastrophic event for a disciple, affecting every aspect of his life. Such a disciple risks the disintegration of his belief (*'aqīda*), both intellectually and spiritually, and may even stray from Islam. The seeker must hold steadfastly to his *wird*, despite being assailed by doubts at various stages of his spiritual journey. Furthermore, the disciple should pray to Allah ﷻ for the correction of his belief, or else he is headed for ruin.

The Shaykh's teachings are pivotal in renewing the disciple's faith and invigorating his progression on the path of Truth. These teachings target the flaws impeding his spiritual journey, propelling the disciple toward the highest echelons of *wilāya* (sainthood). Thus, while *dhikr* is an optional practice in Islam, it becomes mandatory upon *bay'a*, as the disciple commits to Allah, the Prophet ﷺ, and the Shaykh—the bearer of the Prophet's secret. The Qur'ān, with Allah's command, stresses the importance of honoring commitments. In *Sūra* al-Naḥl, verse 91, it is stated: **"Honor Allah's covenant when you have pledged it, and do not break your oaths after affirming them, having made Allah your witness; verily, Allah knows what you do."**

The disciple ought to feel shame for not honoring his commitment. A concerning issue is that numerous disciples neglect this duty and yet have the audacity to appear before the Shaykh—may Allah sanctify his secret. On the Day of Judgment, however, such hypocrisy will prove useless, as the Shaykh will bear witness against each one. Each *wird* (litany) is recorded, and those who have missed even a single *wird* will face consequences. Disciples who have abandoned their *wird* will deeply regret their lack of commitment.

It's important to recognize the Shaykh's mercy towards his disciples; he mandates only two *tasbīḥs* per day, leaving them without excuse before Allah ﷻ on the Day of Judgment. Those who forsake their *wird* should realize that it is Allah ﷻ who relinquishes them, not vice versa. Committing to the Shaykh equates to a commitment to the entirety of creation, encompassing the seven heavens, the seven earths, the Throne (*'arsh*), and the Pedestal (*kursī*). Anyone who abandons his *wird* will be accountable to every element of these realms, as he will claim his rights. These wrongdoers will be deprived of everything. Allah ﷻ is the Mighty One (*al-'Azīz*) and the entire creation zealously guards His honor. Thus, those who fail in his commitments must beware. A true disciple harbors a constant fear of even slightly deviating from his commitments and is always alert to avoid the snares of the *nafs* (ego) and Shayṭān (Satan).

The disciple who relayed the interpreted dream initially neglected her *wird*, then removed her headscarf, although it is an ordained obligation by Allah ﷻ in His *sharīʿa*, symbolizing modesty and protection. Later, she began greeting men with handshakes, a practice strictly prohibited in Islam and previously not followed by her. The Prophet ﷺ never engaged in handshakes with women. Her justification was the discomfort of being judged for wearing the veil; this led to her spiritual faltering. Those who waver under human scrutiny and transgress Allah's prohibitions lack firm principles.

This disciple must understand that everything that is happening to her is the consequence of failing in her obligations to Allah ﷻ.

What should a disciple do to honor his commitments? The path is to adhere to the family of the Prophet ﷺ not out of initial affection but out of a sense of duty, irrespective of personal feelings. Affection will develop over time. The Prophet ﷺ stated: "I leave behind the *thaqalayn* (two weighty things): the Book of Allah and my Family, the People of my House. The Gentle One (Allah) has informed me that they will not part until they rejoin me at the Pool (until the Day of Judgment). Be mindful of how you treat them after me." Disciples must also remember that Islam mandates the fulfillment of commitments at all costs until life's end. Islam is a noble faith, and Muslims must embody the virtues of their religion.

*

How to Cure Hypocrisy

A disciple inquires: How can I rid myself of the hypocrisy ingrained in me by society and my upbringing? Is this hypocrisy the result of the evil eye, sorcery, or greed?

The seeker must recognize that the root of this issue lies within his own *nafs* (soul); it's the outcome of personal thoughts. True, sorcery and greed are real, but the seeker should remember that the influence of *shayṭān* (Satan) is quite weak, as the Holy Qur'ān mentions. He should also understand that a sorcerer can never triumph, regardless of his or her location. Allah ﷻ states in *Sūra* Ṭā-Hā, verse 69: **"What they have conjured up is merely a magician's trick; and the magician will not thrive, no matter where he goes."**

One should internally dismiss these vices as non-existent, ignore them to rest his intellect, and stop thinking about them. One should always view his parents positively, irrespective of his personality. The seeker should also realize that the vices leading to his downfall originate not from others but from within himself. This principle is echoed in the Qur'ān, *Sūra* al-Nisā', verse 79: "Whatever good you receive is from Allah, and whatever evil befalls you is from yourself."

The reality is this disciple has always adapted like a chameleon to attain worldly goals and desires. Evil should always be seen as emanating from one's ego and soul. The Prophet ﷺ describes the traits of a hypocrite in a hadith reported by al-Bukhārī and Muslim ؓ in their *Ṣaḥīḥ*. As per Abd Allāh ibn 'Amr ؓ the Prophet ﷺ stated: "Whoever possesses these four traits is a complete hypocrite, and anyone who has any of these traits has an aspect of hypocrisy until it is abandoned: Betrayal when entrusted, lying when speaking, being treacherous in agreements, and acting rudely and insultingly in disputes."

This indicates that a hypocrite is fundamentally a liar, failing to honor commitments made to the Lord. Additionally, a person who resorts to insults, physical aggression, and who unleashes his filthy darkness during a debate exhibits traits of hypocrisy. Betraying trusts is another characteristic of a hypocrite.

The Prophet ﷺ has provided remedies to cure hypocrisy: when a Muslim commits, he must honor his commitment as the Qur'ān dictates (like the commitment to the *wird* in Allah's Path), or else it's a betrayal of the Prophet ﷺ.

A Muslim must refrain from lying. The Prophet ﷺ advised: "Speak good or remain silent!" Good, in this context, means speaking the truth.

If a believer entrusts us with a deposit and we agree to take it on, we must act responsibly towards it in the sight of Allah ﷻ and never neglect it. Similarly, as instructed by the Prophet ﷺ we should love him more than our own selves, our wealth, our children, and our parents. This responsibility must never be neglected.

One who becomes enraged in a debate and fails to control his anger should redo his ablutions, and if insufficient, perform *ghusl* (full ablution) with cold water, reciting the prayer of the Beloved ﷺ: "O Allah, cleanse me of my sins with water, snow, and ice."

Those who follow these pieces of advice will heal from hypocrisy and remove it from his hearts. This will impact all members of his family, for just as he might have been the cause of their decline, his new behavior, in accordance with the directives of the Prophet ﷺ will be the cause of their prosperity.

*

When You Come to the *Walī*, You Embark on a Migration Towards Allah

In a dream, a woman inquires whether the Shaykh can transcend distances to pray at the Ka'ba.

Disciples must realize that for the Shaykh, the easiest task is to transcend time and space, thus moving freely throughout creation.

Those who believe they have reached the *walī* through their own *nafs* (self) have misunderstood the essence of *wilāya* (sainthood). The journey to reach the Vicegerent of God, though it seems to follow a causal chain, is in reality facilitated only by the grace of Allah ﷻ and with the *idhn* (permission) of the *walī*. This principle also applies to past *awliyā'* (saints). We can visit them posthumously only with their *idhn*.

Anyone desiring to visit the Shaykh must adhere to the principles of *adab* (proper etiquette) in his approach.

First and foremost, we need to understand that visiting the *walī* is akin to migrating towards Allah ﷻ. Such a migration is far from trivial.

It's important for disciples to recognize that the early companions made their migration from Mecca to Medina using their own means. Therefore, one should embark on this migration with his own funds; relying on others' contributions inevitably leads to their association in one's spiritual journey towards Allah ﷻ. Resorting to subterfuges, like claiming that the money was received as a gift, is ineffective. The ideal way to migrate towards the Shaykh is to work and earn one's own money with the intention of funding this unique journey. The purpose of this migration should be the disciple's liberation from *dunyā* (worldly life), vices, and passions.

Tajrīd (detachment) stands as a principal foundation of the stay in the *Zāwiya* (Sufi lodge). A disciple who arrives at the *Zāwiya* but remains tethered to worldly life or passions exhibits a belief deficiency. In reality, such a person does not fully embrace the *shahāda* (testimony of faith, *lā ilāha illā Allah*), which unequivocally declares that there is no deity but Allah ﷻ. The passions to which one clings are illusory; the more one indulges in them, the more they inadvertently associate these with Allah ﷻ.

Session III
October 18, 2020

*

Swimming in the Two Seas: The Sea of *Sharīʿa* and the Sea of *Ḥaqīqa*

A disciple dreamt he had transformed into an aquatic creature, living in a serene and crystal-clear sea. He felt a profound sense of well-being in this water.

The sea, where the disciple immerses and loses himself, is merely a small part of the vast ocean of his Shaykh. In *Sūra* al-Raḥmān, Allah ﷻ states: **"The two seas meet at a barrier/an isthmus (*barzakh*), yielding pearls and corals"**. These two seas represent the sea of *sharīʿa* and the sea of *ḥaqīqa* (Truth).

For Allah's followers, *sharīʿa* is like the land, whereas *ḥaqīqa* resembles the sea. On further contemplation, one realizes that beneath the sea's surface lies the land. Likewise, on land, there is water in rivers, lakes, etc., and deep within the earth, groundwater exists. Therefore, what resides in the sea is also present on land.

Allah ﷻ thus illustrates that there is no true separation between *sharīʿa* and *ḥaqīqa*. The esoteric sciences originate from the exoteric sciences, and the converse is also true. This distinction is simply a product of human intellect. It is crucial to recognize that all was created to lead us back to Allah ﷻ.

In Islamic jurisprudence, the sea is considered pure, and thus everything within it (minerals, life forms, etc.) is pure and fit for consumption. It is a repository of treasures. Sayyidunā ʿUmar ﷺ advised: "Teach your children to swim (*sibāḥa*)," a teaching he likely drew from the Prophet ﷺ.

Given that each utterance of the Prophet ﷺ carries an esoteric meaning, the act of swimming here symbolizes immersing oneself (*tasbīḥ*) in both the exoteric and esoteric seas of knowledge, thereby navigating through Allah's *malakūt*.

The sea makes up seventy percent of Earth, with the remainder being land. To attain *ḥaqīqa*, one must swim through the seven recitations of the Supreme Name, Allah. *Sharīʿa* would thus be encompassed in the remaining three recitations of the Name. Those who successfully unite *ḥaqīqa* and *sharīʿa* will be bestowed with unlimited treasures, the pearls and corals of wisdom.

Allah ﷻ mentions in *Sūra* al-Raḥmān: **"From these two [seas] emerge pearls and corals"**. A seeker can truly claim to be within *sharīʿa* or *ḥaqīqa* only upon experiencing them. However, the sea's flavor is salty and bitter. To drink from these two waters, one must undertake *mujāhada* (spiritual struggle), and thus the seeker becomes an aquatic entity, capable of swimming in both seas.

*

Separation (*faṣl*): Bridging *Sharīʿa* and *Ḥaqīqa*

The separation (*faṣl*) in the Name of Allah ﷻ lies in the empty space between the *alif* and the *lām* of knowledge. This void in the spiritual journey serves as the bridge connecting *sharīʿa* and *ḥaqīqa*, akin to the *barzakh* (intermediary realm) between two seas. The seeker is tasked with being both the unifier and the separator of these two seas, a role only a *walī* (saint) can fulfill.

To attain this station, the seeker must emulate water, as water is transparent to everything. He must thus shed any unnecessary excess within himself.

One who is steadfast in *mujāhada* (spiritual struggle) will succeed in reaching this station, becoming capable of flowing through all things. Such a person will discover water even within a stone. Despite a stone's outwardly dry and barren appearance, it secretly harbors water.

In a similar vein, *sharīʿa*, when viewed externally, may seem rigid. However, if a disciple applies it diligently and in detail, he will realize that it, too, is imbued with water. Persistence in delving deep into the earth, akin to meticulous adherence to *sharīʿa*, will eventually cause water to spring forth. Thus, from such rigid earth, fluid water emerges. The individual who pursues *sharīʿa* in this manner will experience the true essence of the exoteric sciences and be able to "swim" through all of God's creation.

*

The Enlightened by Allah
and the Astray in Philosophy

A Sufi who strays from the *sharīʿa* has not truly grasped the spiritual journey or the teachings of the Prophet ﷺ. The *sharīʿa* represents the sunna of the Prophet ﷺ manifested in this world through his actions and sayings. In fact, the *sharīʿa* is akin to the breath of the Prophet ﷺ. Those who claim to arrive at the truth without adhering to the *sharīʿa* are in grave contradiction. This deviation, often seen in philosophy, leads its followers to erroneously accept following Buddhists, Christians, or Jews as paths to *ḥaqīqa*. Such misguided individuals exist and are, indeed, heretics. These dark ideologies, imported from the West, advocate for a union of all religions and assert the validity of all dogmas.

Why are those who subscribe to this ideology heretical? They essentially reject the *sharīʿa*, which is the sole gateway to truth within the teachings of Prophet Muhammad ﷺ.

There is no path to truth other than that of Our Lord and our Beloved Prophet Muhammad ﷺ. Regrettably, some disciples carry this base heresy. A disciple, once deeply misguided, informed me that he had started studying Buddhism to integrate it into the Tariqa. We clarified to him that, in reality, he was immersing himself in the disbelief inherent in Buddhism.

Those who resonate with such thoughts must understand that Buddhism is not a religion of Allah ﷻ but merely philosophy. Buddhism cannot lead to the secrets of Allah ﷻ, as *tawḥīd* has only one gateway, previously mentioned, which is Islam through our lord and master Muhammad ﷺ.

Those following Buddhism will inevitably collide with the doctrines of incarnation and union (*al-ḥulūl wa-l-it-tiḥād*), mistakenly believing that God intermingles with His creation, whereas Allah ﷻ is transcendent above such impurity. The true Sufi is he who follows the path of his Lord, attains the spiritual vision of the Light, and dissolves his ephemeral self in the Real (*al-Ḥaqq*). This wayfarer need not fear the misconceptions of incarnation and union. Disciples who boast of learning such errors as Buddhism should realize their utter disrespect towards the lineage of the Prophet ﷺ as they delve deeper into disbelief and polytheism, and should refrain from deceiving us with their falsehoods and lies.

However, disciples studying philosophy in the tradition of Imam al-Ghazālī ﷺ are not misled by Shayṭān, as they recognize the fallacies in their studies. They engage in such studies only to demonstrate the limitations of this field compared to the knowledge of Allah ﷻ. Imam al-Ghazālī ﷺ advocated for understanding and internalizing the viewpoints of opponents before rebutting them.

One should never pride oneself on philosophical pursuits. Philosophy is inherently flawed, and any thought process not derived from the *dhikr* of Allah ﷻ is illicit.

Philosophy goes beyond the boundaries of *sharī'a*, and any reflection and intellection devoid of *dhikr* is futile. Still, even futile *dhikr* is preferable to contravening the *sharī'a*. Allah ﷻ states in *Sūra* Āl-'Imrān, verse 191: **"Those who remember Allah, standing, sitting, and lying on their sides, and reflect on the creation of the heavens and the earth."**

A disciple who studies philosophy with a correct belief recognizes the misguidance of his studies, unlike those who delve into Buddhism and other philosophies, thinking they contain hidden truths. There is an enormous gulf between those enlightened by authentic *'aqīda* (creed) and those attempting to align Buddhism, Christianity, or any other misguided belief with the Tariqa.

Followers of philosophy should be aware that the extent of their knowledge is limited to the senses and faculties of the perishable body. Aspiring to transcend these limitations is strictly forbidden for them. The divine realm, the realm of the Spirit, will forever remain an enigma to them.

As long as a disciple experiences existence through his body rather than through his heart, he remains astray. He will constantly be ensnared in the illusions of incarnation and union. We tirelessly emphasize that the Real, the True Existent, can never merge and mix with the non-existent. Returning to the truth of the Real, we persistently declare that one must annihilate oneself by following the path delineated by the Prophet ﷺ, which is the exclusive route of the blessed *sharīʿa*. This pursuit must be undertaken without overstepping its bounds. This path stands as the sole portal to Allah ﷻ shielding those seeking knowledge from the misguided paths of philosophers and heretical, self-styled mystics.

*

The Love of Allah

A disciple had a dream where he was going to the mosque of Sayyidunā Ḥusayn (Cairo) during the time of the fajr prayer. Entry was initially denied due to the Coronavirus. However, he received a mystical call (hātif) from Sayyidunā Ḥusayn, granting him permission to enter, which he did without encountering any further obstacles.

A disciple cannot impose his love on the people of Allah ﷻ. Even if he proclaims his love for them, it can never equal the love of the people of Allah ﷻ for him. The disciple must understand that any love he holds for the people of Allah ﷻ is solely a grace from Allah ﷻ. The disciple has done nothing to deserve this love.

The mere ability to perform prayer is a divine gift. Those who do not cherish prayer, pray infrequently, or engage little in *dhikr*, must realize they are neglected by their Lord, not vice versa.

It is important to recognize that the good fortune a disciple experiences is also channeled through the people of Allah ﷻ. Furthermore, whoever does not frequently pray upon the Prophet ﷺ and his family should realize he has not been granted permission to do so. Truly, we can only call upon those whom Allah ﷻ loves when Allah ﷻ loves us. Similarly, we can only be united with the *awliyā'* when they permit us. Should a disciple be called upon by them, he will come by any means necessary, even if it means crawling.

To illustrate this point, let's consider some residents of Medina who have never visited the Prophet's mosque despite its proximity. When questioned about their absence from the mosque, they might attribute it to a lack of diligence. In truth, it is because Allah ﷻ does not favor them. Visiting the Prophet is a virtue, and all virtue originates from Allah ﷻ and His Messenger ﷺ.

Take the example of Sayyidunā Ibrahim ﷺ, who is beloved by Allah ﷻ. He asked Allah ﷻ to demonstrate how He resurrects the dead. Allah ﷻ questioned his belief, to which Sayyidunā Ibrahim ﷺ responded that he sought reasSūrance for his heart. One of the greatest manifestations of Allah's love is the fulfillment of a servant's prayers. Here, Ibrahim ﷺ sought the Knowledge of Resurrection. As instructed by his Lord, he went to four mountains, sacrificed four birds, mixed them, and placed parts on each mountain. Then Allah ﷻ commanded him to call the birds, and they came to him, reassembled.

This story shows that when chosen by Allah's grace one will humbly and earnestly seek His presence, even if it requires crawling. To determine if we are among such blessed individuals, we should introspect. For instance, do we approach the mosque at the call to prayer in a state of humility and with a soul yearning for purification? Or do we invent excuses, such as work or fatigue? This simple reflection reveals one's true self and spiritual status.

In our poetry collection *"Diwān ul-Dīnān,"* we say: "The Real called me up from my paradise (his heart), and Knowledge began to flow through my Tongue; He who loved me has guided me."

Allah ﷻ has bestowed upon us the privilege to elevate from the heart and to disseminate the True sciences. This achievement is solely by the grace of the Beloved Prophet ﷺ. To calm our spirits like Ibrahim ﷺ we delved into the contemplation of the Sun of the Prophet ﷺ. Our hearts, cleared of idols, became receptive to the wisdom of Al-Muṣṭafā ﷺ and the knowledge of the Divine. Thus, those who believe they hold divine knowledge or understanding simply because they are familiar with the stories of philosophers like Socrates, Thales, or Pythagoras are actually harboring only an illusion of knowledge. Indeed, philosophy alone does not constitute the essence of true knowledge.

Consider Imam al-Ghazālī ﵀, a distinguished scholar in the exoteric sciences of Islam, who, upon reaching a state of spiritual emptiness, chose to renounce all his scholarly works. He came to the profound realization that the truest and most meaningful pursuit was the science of love and matters of the heart.

To achieve the attributes that lead to the love of Allah ﷻ one must immerse himself in the lord's knowledge and strive to emulate our Prophet ﷺ. This stage of spiritual development, known as *takhlia*, involves shedding all preconceived ideas and intellectual obscurities. It is a process of abandoning one's philosophical darkness. Subsequently, the Lord ﷻ adorns us with His attributes and imparts His Divine Science. In conforming to this path, the truth becomes manifest, and the disciple comes to realize *fanā'* (the annihilation of the ego), which is the ultimate aspiration of the Sufi.

Session IV
November 1, 2020

*

The Prophet's Central Role in the *Lām*

In the *huwa* (هـو), the significance lies in the *wāw* (و),
symbolizing the six pillars of *īmān* (faith). The *wāw* embodies the center, source, and truth of the *hā'*, representing
the *maqām* (station) of *al-īmān*. Therefore, for the *hā'* to
realize its full potential, it must dissolve in the *wāw*.

During the second reading of the Name, in the *lām*,
the seeker discerns where Allah ﷻ has positioned His
emanatory source.

At the birth of the Prophet ﷺ a star emerged in the
sky. This star was identified by the rabbis, monks, and
priests of that era. Through their scholarly knowledge,
they recognized that the final Prophet ﷺ had come. They
turned to their scriptures and manuscripts, seeking the
earthly embodiment of this prophecy. In the *lām*, the
disciple channels this passion by internalizing the search
for the Prophet ﷺ.

By diligently following the Shaykh in the study of the *hāʾ*, and annihilating his senses and limbs in his Shaykh, the disciple grasps the Prophet's ﷺ pivotal role. The disciple then perceives that the most luminous star in existence is the Prophet ﷺ and that all other stars are merely reflections of this singular one.

The Prophet's star ﷺ is a beacon leading to unity, encapsulating all Divine attributes and names, whereas other stars are their reflections. These reflect the companions, symbolizing the dispersed Divine Attributes and Names.

When witnessing multiple stars in *mushāhada* (awakened vision), one should seek the brightest star to connect directly with the source, the star that encompasses all. In doing so, the disciple abbreviates his spiritual journey and links directly to the Vicegerent of God, bypassing intermediaries, for there are as many stars as there are intermediaries. One must seek the essence of all stars to bond his heart to it and follow its guidance. This embrace of guidance manifests in only two ways: either through devoted following born out of love for one's Imam, or through compelled adherence driven by the fear of not following.

A hadith from the Prophet ﷺ differentiates between passion (*ʿishq*) and constriction (*qabḍ*). In a hadith in *Ṣaḥīḥ al-Bukhārī*, Sayyidunā Abu Hurayra ﷺ recounts that the Prophet ﷺ told Sayyidunā ʿUmar ﷺ: "You are not a true believer until your love for me surpasses that for your family, your wealth, and your own self (*nafs*)."

Qabḍ involves orienting the heart towards worldly or earthly (*dunya*) matters: family, wealth, or the *nafs*. Conversely, love is found in the pursuit of the Prophet ﷺ and it is this pursuit that gives rise to *'ishq*. The disciple must understand that constriction and passion are intertwined, each one following and accompanying the other.

*

How Can a Disciple Become the Shadow of the Shaykh?

Allah ﷻ tells us in *Sūra* al-Zukhruf, verse 85: "And blessed is He to Whom belongs the dominion of the heavens and the earth, and everything in between."

Allah ﷻ created the heavens and the earth for Himself, the *lahu* (لَهُ). This *lahu* represents the *khalīfa* (Vicegerent), namely the *walī*, who "belongs" entirely to Allah ﷻ.

A seeker can truly become the shadow of the Shaykh, or fulfill their role in the *khilāfa*, only by aligning entirely with the decrees of the *walī*. This means complete surrender to Him, irrespective of the state of constriction (*qabḍ*) the seeker is in.

To comprehend how the disciple will become the shadow of the Shaykh, consider an example from the trace (*athar*) of the circle of *hā' al-huwiyya* (*hā'* of divine identity): If the Shaykh is the center and circumference of the circle of *huwiyya*, then the disciple is akin to a radius within this circle. This radius passes through the center but is not the center itself. The Shaykh will gradually shape the disciple into his image, transforming him into the likeness of the center after purifying him and subsuming all his attributes into his blessed Person. As long as the seeker resides within the realm of the *hā'*, he is akin to a radius connected to the circle's center, exhibiting an affinity and attraction towards the circle's circumference. This condition persists because of his ongoing attachment to the transient.

During the exploration of the *hā'*, the Shaykh situates the disciple in this circle, the Niche. Thus, the disciple begins to witness the things that occur within and perceives the residing Light. Then, the Shaykh merges this niche with his own vision, hearing, and speech. In doing so, the disciple will perceive the Light of *al-Baṣīr* (the All-Seeing), *al-Samī'* (the All-Hearing), and *al-Kalīm* (the Speaker).

Therefore, it's essential to understand that the aspiration of one seeking entry into the *lām* is more profound than the pursuit within the *hā'*. In the *lām*, the disciple is required to extinguish his physical senses, as mentioned in the supplication the Prophet ﷺ recited en route to the mosque.

Besides extinguishing his senses as previously mentioned, the disciple must also extinguish his bodily aspects and directions in the Light: his bones, muscles, skin, blood, and hair, until he becomes the name *al-Nūr* (the Light) itself.

The disciple will thus attain the center and the Supreme Name, as the names have never departed from the named.

In hadiths recorded in the *Ṣaḥīḥ* and the *musnad Aḥmad*, the Prophet ﷺ said: "O Lord! Place in my heart Light, in my tongue Light, in my hearing Light, in my sight Light, beneath me Light, above me Light, to my right Light, to my left Light, in front of me Light, behind me Light, grant me Light, place in my nerves Light, in my flesh Light, in my blood Light, in my hair Light, and in my skin Light, make my *nafs* Light, and sanctify me with this Light."

To guide the disciple toward the *lām*, the Shaykh will initiate him to become the perfect manifestation of the Name Light. This initiation also enables the disciple to grasp the sciences emanating from it.

When the disciple approaches the Shaykh to commit to the path of Allah, the Shaykh prays for him to receive this Light that will lead him to the secrets. The Shaykh will gradually reveal these secrets during the *wird*. In this process, we assist the disciple in his dissolution into this Light through these secrets, allowing him to experience the divine Essence.

In entering *khulwa*, the disciple converges all the universes that Allah ﷻ created from the Light of the rings of the *mishkāt*. He will come to realize that these rings focus into a singular point. When the disciple nullifies these universes, the *lām* of constriction emerges, compelling the disciple to relinquish all distractions, such as children, wealth, and the *nafs*. Sacrifice becomes imperative to enter the *lām*. This is merely the beginning, as in the *lām* of passion the disciple must forsake his immediate surroundings, while in the *lām* of knowledge, or *ma'rifa*, he must relinquish his *nafs* and all the stars he observes in *mushāhada*, remaining solely with the Star of the Shaykh.

Through this constriction, passion is kindled. The more the disciple distances himself from his surroundings, the more intensely he experiences the *lām* of passion, and the more profoundly he savors the Spirit. It is through this process that he "sells" (dedicates) everything to Allah.

*

The Staves of the Shaykh: A *Lām* and an *Alif*

The staff wielded by the Shaykh in the *ḥadra* (Sufi ritual dance) is akin to an *alif*. The *alif*, characterized by its two straight sides that do not bend, represents absolute *istiqāma* (uprightness). This signifies its non-appearance in the transient world. Conversely, the *lām* possesses one end mirroring the *alif's* straightness, while its other end curves, similar to the *hā'*. This curve forms a semi-circle, enabling the *lām* to connect with the transient world.

The *walī* (saint) embodies the *lām* in the name of Allah ﷻ. He epitomizes unparalleled uprightness on one side and manifests in the transient world on the other.

He exists in dual realities: one in the *alif's* transcendence, associated with the Prophet ﷺ, invisible in the transient world, and the other within the transient world itself. Hence, he has a door towards us, who are impure, and a door towards Him, who is pure.

The Shaykh employs the *lām's* staff to connect the disciples, bound by the transient, to the Absolute.

Imbuing the *alif's* staff with spiritual intention, he inscribes Allah's ﷻ Supreme Name at the *ḥadra's* epicenter, effectively the Niche's core. Through this process, disciples gain access to knowledge that transcends mere intellect.

*

The Light of Believers and the Words of Hypocrites

In *Sūra* al-Ḥadīd, verse 12, Allah ﷻ states: **"On the day when you will see the believing men and women, their Light flowing ahead of them and to their right, [they will be told]: 'Today, you have good tidings of Gardens beneath which rivers flow, dwelling therein forever. This is the ultimate success.'"**

The believers join hands, forming a circle. This Light running through their hands fills their entire semi-circle and is only possible after their purification. These individuals have realized themselves in the *hā'*. In contrast to the "hypocrites," who remain caught up in mere vain speeches and the superficial.

Then, Allah ﷻ continues in *Sūra* al-Ḥadīd, verse 13: **"On the day when the hypocritical men and women will say to the believers: 'Wait for us, let us have some of your Light.' It will be said: 'Go back to your rear (the dunya) and seek light!' Then, a wall with a gate will be** erected between them. Inside it, there is mercy, and outside, facing it, lies torment."

In this scenario, the Light of the believers streams between their shoulders. It is akin to an *alif* or a half-cylinder. Indeed, in the circle of *ḥadra*, believers are illuminated from the front, whereas for those at the back, we no longer speak of believers or the degree of *al-īmān*, i.e. *farq* (differentiation), but rather the Light of union, or *jamʿ*.

The Holy Qur'ān here illustrates the level a believer can attain in the Light. In this verse, believers and hypocrites coexist in the same space, yet each occupies his distinct *maqām* (spiritual station). The believers instruct the hypocrites to return to the *dunya*—the worldly life— to seek the Light they now desire in the afterlife, underscoring that Light is earned through deeds, not mere words. The *dunya* is the realm where Allah provides opportunities for action. On the Day of Judgment, actions cease to count. Thus, the *dunya* is a field where we sow for what we will reap later. This field must be cultivated with good seeds to yield sweet fruits in the hereafter. This final abode is where accounts are settled, and there are neither deeds nor labors. The wall separating believers and hypocrites, as described, signifies that even in the same space, as the earlier part of the verse indicates, a division will exist. Allah ﷻ prohibits hypocrites from residing amongst believers. This wall represents the divide between these two groups, erected when the hypocrites approach the believers. This demonstrates that the words of the hypocrites will lead them to scission.

In contrast, the words of the believers shine with Light, as they are always engaged in either *dhikr* or showing compassion towards others. In the inner being (*bāṭin*) of a believer resides the Mercy of Allah ﷻ, the wellspring of Light. The believer's words, stemming from a *bāṭin* filled with mercy, attract thus both angels and the Mercy of Allah ﷻ. Conversely, the words of hypocrites attract nothing but sins and demons.

Sayyidunā 'Alī ؓ emphasizes this point by saying: "If someone speaks in our presence, we can discern his true nature within the hour by his speech." The *awliyā'* (saints) indeed can distinguish hypocrites from believers quickly by their words.

One who does not dedicate time to spreading words on the path leading to the Most Merciful's Door, aspiring to be among the believers, will inevitably devote his time to worldly pursuits and the haunts of hypocrites and *shayṭāns*. Such a person is doomed to mislead his own soul. The Door of the Most Merciful is none other than the Vicegerent, whose identity varies with the times. He may be a Prophet, a Messenger, or a *walī* of Allah ﷻ.

*

The Trial of Doubt: The Road to Hypocrisy

Allah ﷻ states in *Sūra* al-Ḥadīd, verse 14: "[The hypocrites inquire]: Were we not with you? they will call out. Yes, [the believers] will respond, but you succumbed to the temptations of your *nafs* (in *fitna*), conspired (against the believers), and were plagued by doubt. False hopes misled you until Allah's decree arrived. And the deceiver (the devil/*nafs*) beguiled you about Allah."

Allah ﷻ explains that the hypocrites fell into *fitna*, harbored doubts, and even conspired against the believers. Why? They lost their way because, rather than perceiving the believers with a forgiving eye that prevents doubts, they chose to focus on their faults. We cannot harbor doubts about someone if we maintain a positive view of them. Concentrating on their flaws leads to doubts arising. Had the hypocrites looked upon the believers with mercy, they would have never doubted or conspired against them. Their reluctance to embrace the truth is rooted in this doubt and *fitna*, resulting in their misguidedness.

*

The Misguidance of Neo-Sufis

Allah ﷻ mentions in *Sūra* al-Ḥadīd, verse 16: "Has the time not arrived for the believers that their hearts should be softened with the remembrance of Allah and the truth that has descended?"

This verse suggests that not all believers can achieve complete realization in the presence of the Light. Among them, the neo-Sufis, possess the knowledge of *īmān* but do not harness this *īmān* to fear Allah ﷻ. Some of these individuals persist in following deceased Shaykhs.

Further in the verse, Allah ﷻ warns: **"And be not like those who received the Scripture before, and a long period passed over them, so their hearts hardened; many of them are transgressors."**

These individuals must awaken to avoid following the path of the People of the Book. Prophets were sent to *ahl al-kitāb* to guide them to the Muhammadan truth, to follow Prophet Muhammad ﷺ. Yet, they chose not to. They continue to adhere to the old messengers and prophets to this day.

This is where the neo-Sufis of today draw a parallel, who, rather than adhering to a living Shaykh, the representative of their era, the connector between the servant and his Lord, cling to masters no longer alive. If these people overlook the *walī* of their era, their hearts will harden, and many will become corrupt, as the aforementioned verse indicates. This is akin to the *ahl al-kitāb* who neglected to follow the Beloved Messenger of Allah ﷺ.

Every Muslim, therefore, must strive to discover the Gate of Mercy, namely the *walī* of his time, who will guide him towards Allah ﷻ.

Upon finding him, he must fully surrender while striving to quell his *nafs* in his presence. Only through this approach will he achieve fulfillment in the *lām* of the name and grasp the underlying mercy. He will then truly understand the sciences within the *hā'* of Islam and the *wāw* of *īmān*.

Bear in mind, O disciple, that for one who has entered the *ka'ba* (one who has extinguished in the Center, the *walī*), the *ṭawāf* (circumambulation) is no longer a necessity.

Session V
November 2, 2020

*

The Perfection of Ādam's Vessel

The vessel, which is the body or the physical image of Sayyidunā Ādam ﷺ encloses the Throne of the Spirit and the Divine Names. This is why, in the Qur'ān, Allah ﷻ commands the angels to prostrate before Sayyidunā Ādam.

The clay that constitutes Ādam comes directly from Allah ﷻ, for He created him directly with His Hand. Thus, it encompasses the Secrets of the Names of Allah ﷻ and is the Throne of Allah's Secrets.

This clay was created with the utmost precision (*aḥsani taqwīm*). From this perfect source came the descendants of Ādam ﷺ and yet, imperfections appeared in some of his children. The physical image of Sayyidunā Ādam had perfect balance, as is also the case with the Prophets and *awliyā'* (saints) who came after him.

This perfection in the clay conceals the Secrets of Allah ﷻ. It thus aided Sayyidunā Ādam in attaining knowl-

73

edge of Allah's perfection. To reiterate, this vessel (Ādam) is the throne in which Allah's secrets were deposited. The same was true for Sayyidunā 'Alī.

It should also be noted that we are not talking about muscular strength here, but rather about the perfect balance of the four elements: fire, water, air, and earth.

One who possesses this balance in the four elements can journey among the different tablets of the Divine Names. He can understand the gathering of the Names. And it is in this vessel (which has a perfect balance among the four elements) that the seventy secrets can be transmitted.

At the beginning of the journey, when we decided to impart the Supreme Name of Allah ﷻ to our disciples, we chose the four best among them, those who stood out for their sacrifice in the journey towards Allah.

To impart this Name to them, we used the method of the tablet, as was the case with Shaykh al-'Alawī ﵃.

To create a tablet for each, we chose the best carpenter, not in terms of carpentry, and the best bookbinder, not in terms of the quality of materials, but in terms of fear and sincerity towards Allah. These individuals did not even want a salary for their work. Each tablet represented one of the four disciples and also one of the four elements.

It was through these tablets that the disciples journeyed towards *khulwa* (spiritual seclusion) at the beginning of their path.

When Allah decided to create Ādam صلى الله عليه وسلم, He ﷻ also selected the finest of the earth. This is referenced in the Qur'ān, in *Sūra* al-Raḥmān, verse 14: **"He created man from sounding clay, like pottery."**

*

What Is "the Clay Resonant as Pottery"?

The vessel of Sayyidunā Ādam صلى الله عليه وسلم is, let us recall, perfect. It is the Throne of Secrets and Names of Allah ﷻ. These Secrets also emanate from him. Regardless of the disciples' opinions, the angels prostrated before this clay. Allah ﷻ did not command, "Prostrate before Ādam's Light." He directly ordered: **"Prostrate to Ādam"**. Some exoteric scholars attempted to interpret this as meaning, "Prostrate before the Light of Allah ﷻ." However, this interpretation is incorrect, as the Qur'ānic text clearly indicates. The prostration was directly to this clay, as it is perfect. Those unconvinced should refer back to the Holy Qur'ān for their own verification of what Allah ﷻ has stated.

This clay, akin to pottery, is always found near freshwater sources. Its notable characteristics are its moldability and softness, making it ideal for pottery. Allah ﷻ collected earth from near every water source to create Sayyidunā Ādam. Therefore, his creation followed that of the earth.

Disciple, you should know that the number of pores on our skin corresponds to the number of water sources on earth. Allah ﷻ took a drop of water from each source. This earth, made of clay, varies in color from white to black. It also possesses different complexions. It is this diversity that gives rise to various ethnicities.

Thus, in observing populations with darker skin, like African populations, one can note that the nearby water sources are similarly dark (black). In contrast, European populations, with lighter skin, are situated near lighter (white) water sources.

Allah ﷻ did not solely create humanity from clay. If that were so, humans would dissolve in the rain. Instead, Allah ﷻ infused the clay with some heat, turning it into a compact mass. This endows the skin with an equilibrium that enables it to withstand different climatic conditions, preventing it from dissolving in rain or hardening in intense heat.

Water is also crucial in the composition of humans. Rain serves as a purifier for the earth, as exemplified in the story of Prophet Nūḥ ﷺ. Allah ﷻ cleansed the earth where he resided through a flood. Similarly, water also purifies humans. It is indeed necessary to perform full ablutions or *ghusl* after major impurity, *janāba*. Neglecting *ghusl* inadvertently clogs skin pores. In the Malikī rite, it is thus mandatory for water to reach all body parts during ablution.

Allah ﷻ also created other beings named *al-khān*, *al-ḥān*, and *al-jān* before Sayyidunā Ādam. These beings deviated from the righteous path and eventually vanished. Humans are not much different; at the end of times, they, too, will deviate and subsequently perish.

*

The Earth as a Reflection of Humanity: The Maghrib as its Heart

If one seeks to locate a place on Earth endowed with a perfect balance of elements, attention must turn to North Africa, more precisely, the Maghrib. Despite our customary view of the Earth as a globe in geographical maps, it actually mirrors a human being in reality. It possesses a face, hands, and so on. The part representing the chest aligns with the Maghrib. The middle portion, akin to the belly, corresponds to the equator, the warmest zone on Earth. This is not coincidental, as this zone is also the warmest part of the human body. Allah ﷻ also inscribed His Name in North Africa because this region is the best and the most optimal on Earth.

When stating that the Earth genuinely resembles a human being, one should endeavor to transcend the typical image that has been instilled in our consciousness. Similarly, Allah ﷻ mentions in the Qur'ān that mountains move, though our perception sees them as fixed. This doesn't imply that the mountains are immobile, but that the observer's perception is limited, trapped in a static image.

Focusing on the inscription of the Name Allah ﷻ in North Africa, it's important to recognize that the mark of the *hā'* of the Name Allah ﷻ is located at al-Qarawiyyīn in the city of Fes in Morocco. The *lām* is found at the grand Zaytūna Mosque in Tunis, Tunisia. The other *lām* is associated with al-Azhar in Egypt, and the *alif* is in Saudi Arabia, at Madīna, in the Prophet's Mosque, for Madīnah is the city of sciences (*madīnat al-ʿilm*). The dot is manifested by the Ka'ba, namely Makkah.

Thus, the Supreme Name is written exclusively in regions populated by olive trees.

Olive trees are ubiquitous in North Africa, as this area corresponds to the chest (*ṣadr*) or heart of the Earth. It is not a mere coincidence that Allah ﷻ refers to the Blessed Olive Tree in the verse of Light (*Sūra* al-Nūr, verse 35). Allah ﷻ did this to reveal where His Supreme Name is concealed and the place where His *awliyā'*, those who will teach it, will emerge.

*

The *Siyāḥa* in the Body: Multiple Points of Entry, the Heart as the Sole Point of Arrival

As previously noted, Allah ﷻ took this clay from nearby water sources and then created a *khalīfa* (Vicegerent) in His image. Although the *khalīfa* appeared after the Earth's creation, the latter was created in his likeness. When Sayyidunā Ādam ﷺ descended to earth, he landed in

India and began searching for his *nafs*, which is none other than his wife: our mother Ḥawwā' (Eve, ﷵ). She embarked on the same journey. This quest was the first pilgrimage by Man on earth. The couple reunited on Mount *'Arafāt*.

This story shows that women too can undertake pilgrimage. However, this was not entirely true then, as Earth was inhabited solely by Sayyidunā Ādam and our mother Ḥawwā'. It was their domain, allowing Ḥawwā' to traverse safely. Now, with the Earth's dense population and men's competition for women, their safety from misadventure is not ensured. Hence, *siyāḥa* is prohibited for women.

Revisiting the meeting of our Mother Ḥawwā' and Sayyidunā Ādam, they met on Mount *'Arafāt*. *'Arafa* means knowledge, obtained only through the spiritual heart. The globe's center, or heart, is thus at *'Arafāt*, in Mecca. This center should not be equated with that on a current geographical map; otherwise, it might be placed in Tripoli, Libya, given our previous assertion that the globe's chest was in North Africa. In truth, the chest's center or focal point is Mecca, where the heart's secrets and the finest water source, *Zamzam*, reside.

This is why the Prophet ﷺ explains that the *niyya* (intention) accompanying the drinking of *Zamzam* water manifests in the physical realm. *Zamzam* is akin to the Lamp, with other water sources as its reflections in the Niche (*mishkāt*). Earthly formations follow this pattern, comprising a source (*aṣl*) and its reflections. Humans mirror this rule, resembling a globe with its brightest source/lamp at the heart's center, their personal *Zamzam*, and a body resembling a labyrinth of niches reflecting this source. The *nafas* (celestial breath) of the Messenger of Allah ﷺ conceals the treasure of these niches and this Lamp. His grace made *siyāḥa* accessible to all believers in the first heaven, along with the understanding of its treasures.

Indeed, the *siyāḥa* in these heavens occurs within believers' bodies, as the Divine Names and Attributes constitute their bodies' truth. A believer's body thus becomes Allah's Names' throne, as stated in the hadith: "Neither my lands nor my heavens contain Me, only the heart of my believing servant." Through this devout heart, Sayyidunā Ādam encompassed all the Names. While feasible for believers, this is not so for Muslims in the *maqām* (station) of *al-islām*, nor for unbelievers. The *umma's bāṭin* (inner essence) houses its source, with its outward appearance merely containing this truth.

A hadith narrates that Sayyidunā Ādam was created sixty cubits tall. Although his size appears larger than the Prophet's ﷺ, our Beloved reached *al-muntahā* while Ādam ﷺ stayed in the first heaven. This indicates that the Prophet ﷺ reality reaches this *maqām*, though his physical stature is less than Sayyidunā Ādam's.

To illustrate this, consider an example: the earliest computers created were enormous. Over time, they were refined, and their size decreased. Sayyidunā Ādam ﷺ, manifesting the first prophetic image, was tall. Following this, the journey proceeded from one prophet to another, culminating in perfection embodied by the stature of our Prophet Muhammad ﷺ. His community thus mirrors his image. Indeed, as we draw nearer to the spirit, the physical body diminishes, for the spirit is subtle.

This body forms a labyrinth, as previously mentioned. To understand it, one must strive to find its entrance. When disciples come to *bay'a*, each does so with a specific intention. It is this intention that designates the part through which they can comprehend their body. One disciple may find their entrance through their eyes, another through their nose, and so on. These entrances serve as entry points. If a disciple sincerely comes for Allah ﷻ their entry point must be their eye (*'ayn*). If they approach with ill intent, they might enter through a lower part (*suflī*).

Regardless, the role of the Shaykh is to guide the disciple toward the Source, that is, the heart. Foremost, the disciple must find the Gate of all gates, the Shaykh. Without the Shaykh, the disciple can never navigate the labyrinth that is the body. Without the Shaykh, the disciple will never find their gate, nor reach the heart, because it bears repeating: this gate is unique, it is the accomplished Shaykh.

Let no disciple imagine themselves to be the Gate. To understand how the Shaykh guides a disciple through their body, it is essential to know that all points of the body are interconnected through blood vessels, which, in turn, are all connected to the heart. The task of the accomplished Shaykh is to navigate the disciple through their body via these vessels until they reach their heart. Once there, they can experience the secret that Allah ﷻ has instilled in them. This secret is indeed the source for the disciple. This secret is their *Zamzam*.

This is why Allah ﷻ says in *Sūra* Ash-Shuʿarāʾ, verse 89: **"The one who will be saved is the one who comes to Allah with a sound heart."** This is the rationale behind dubbing this discipline as the science of the dot. Indeed, there are multiple entry points, but the point of arrival is unique. Our body is replete with sources and points. The seeker enters through one of these points or sources to reach the point of knowledge located in their heart.

Session VI
November 11, 2020

*

Optimizing One's Visit to the *Zāwiya*

A disciple dreams of visiting the Zāwiya without bringing a gift for Sidi Shaykh.

One who arrives at the *Zāwiya* should sanctify this visit and consider it a migration towards the Real (*al-Ḥaqq*). Indeed, the intention that the disciple seals before his visit to the *Zāwiya* will be crucial in his spiritual journey. If the intention is deviant, he will have a bad stay and will not reap the fruits that a seeker of knowledge could gather. Practically, every disciple in renunciation (*tajrīd*) must constantly review his intention, as often as possible. He must also exercise greater control over his heart and limbs here than in any other place, doing so as frequently as three hundred and sixty times a day. He should question every step he intends to take: does it align with the journey, yes or no?

The disciple should know that if his start in the journey is enlightened and fulfilling, his end will be too. And as the *Zāwiya* can be a place of fulfillment for some, it can also represent a veil and a barrier for others. The disciple who comes to the *Zāwiya*, and instead of engaging in *dhikr* and following the Shaykh, gets distracted by his brothers, will stray and veil himself.

Others will try to accumulate information about the journey through the renounced disciples. These, too, are veiling themselves, for knowledge is not a matter of gathering information but rather a matter of taste (*dhawq*) and spiritual awakening with the Lord.

It is essential to always ensure the correction of one's intention, and when the disciple listens to his brothers or discusses with them, he must see in them manifestations of the Shaykh and abstract from their physical forms and personalities.

When the disciple goes to the *Zāwiya*, he must ask himself what the purpose of his visit is. Let him who comes for rest at the *Zāwiya* know that there are other more restful places than this, so why does he come? It is not a tourist complex for rest.

Most will say that they have come to know Allah ﷻ. These people must always keep this goal in mind and rethink it more than three hundred and sixty times a day, as we have already indicated. They must align all their actions according to this objective. They must question every gesture they make: does it align with spiritual knowledge (*maʿrifa*) or not?

He who wants to be in constant connection with Allah ﷻ must control his *nafs* at every moment.

The disciple should only associate with another disciple when he sees that he can help him achieve his goal: the knowledge of Allah ﷻ (*ma'rifatu Allah*). Otherwise, he must avoid and flee everything that can distract him from this primary objective.

He who comes to the *Zāwiya* must do so with a heart empty of sciences and devoid of information, for he who comes loaded with his experiences or his science will try to educate others, while he himself comes to be educated. This disciple is in difficulty and even in danger because he takes the role of the Shaykh. He must indeed empty his vessel for the Shaykh to fill it. Whereas he who comes with an empty vessel will see it filled with treasures and secrets.

Remember that Allah ﷻ is jealous and desires your heart to be entirely devoted to Him alone, containing only Him. Know that to flourish in the journey, the Shaykh must cast three hundred and sixty positive glances upon you.

He who admits to never having known his Lord is welcome. The arrival of he who regards the *walī* as the center of the universe through his prophetic heritage is comparable to the *ḥajj*. This disciple must perform the seven circumambulations (*ṭawāf*), starting with the *hā'*, which is the first reading. This initial *ṭawāf* should be performed quickly. Coming to the *Zāwiya* is synonymous with spiritual education and learning, aimed at acquiring knowledge of the Divine. This place is not intended for creating social ties, which some disciples mistakenly do.

Moreover, it is advisable to bring a gift to the Shaykh, as this action benefits the disciple. This gesture, imbued with Light, symbolizes the disciple's effort for his master, undertaken even before entering the blessed enclosure. The disciple who selects a gift must first exert effort in choosing it, effectively placing himself in the Shaykh's position to ascertain the latter's preferences. This act, in and of itself, represents a form of annihilation (*fanā'*) in the Shaykh. Subsequently, he must exert effort to travel and acquire the gift, eventually investing his time and resources to provide it. Unbeknownst to him, the disciple experiences *fanā'* in his Shaykh through these actions, aiming to please the master. Such efforts are a precursor to the sanctification of the educating Shaykh and are beneficial for the disciple's journey, as he will witness many veils being lifted. Conversely, one who arrives impulsively, without a gift, fails to confer the same level of sanctity to the master and may find his progress in the journey hindered. Indeed, the entire journey hinges on the bond the disciple forms with the *wāsiṭa* (intermediary). The stronger this relationship is, the more fruits the disciple will harvest in the journey. Despite these established practices, some individuals remain resistant to these conventions. However, as the beloved Prophet ﷺ stated, "Exchange gifts, and you will love one another."

Allah ﷻ responds to those who dislike these conventions, saying in *Sūra* al-Tawbā, Verse 111: **"Allah has purchased from the *mu'mins* (believers) their *nafs* (souls) and their property in exchange for paradise."**

Everything the disciple offers in the path of Allah ﷻ is there to fulfill this sacred exchange.

Additionally, it is important to note that if the *walī* asks the disciple to prolong his stay in the *Zāwiya*, it is to let him reap the best fruits of his journey. Therefore, he should accept without hesitation. The Shaykh is best positioned to decide on the duration of each disciple's stay. Beyond this period, staying in the *Zāwiya* will not bring even a crumb of knowledge of Allah ﷻ.

The true knower of Allah (*'ārif billāh*) is he who reaches the station of *lillāh* (ﷲ). He does everything for Allah ﷻ and will see all creation prostrate before him because he no longer sees the creation, but rather the One who created it. This disciple will prostrate for the commands of Allah ﷻ and flee from all His prohibitions.

In conclusion, before setting foot in the *Zāwiya*, it is imperative to set an intention directed towards the knowledge of Allah ﷻ (*ma'rifatu Allāh*) and another towards spiritual fulfillment. Let him who comes for something else declare it from the start, for sooner or later, we will unveil it.

*

The Importance of the Group in Monitoring the *Nafs*

A brother shares a dream in which he sees an elderly man among the Karkaris. This man decides to isolate himself from the group, but a voice promptly calls him back.

One harms himself by distancing from the group and seeking isolation. The power and strength in following the Shaykh is rooted in the group. It is within the group that a disciple learns to fear Allah ﷻ. Isolation poses a risk in the spiritual path, particularly for new disciples susceptible to vices. Many prohibitions that might be ignored in solitude are respected in the group, where individuals would feel ashamed to engage in them.

*

Prostrate to Him, and the Mountains Will Follow

The Prophet ﷺ depicted the *sirāṭ al-mustaqīm* (straight path) as thinner than a hair and sharper than a razor blade. This description is employed to emphasize the necessity of unceasing vigilance over one's *nafs*. Nonetheless, despite such scrupulous oversight, a disciple might find himself momentarily distracted by his surroundings.

A crucial point in one's spiritual journey comes when the disciple recognizes that his sincere efforts in supervising and controlling the *nafs* are not a result of personal merit. This realization is accompanied by the understanding that it is fundamentally Allah's mercy at play. Such a disciple becomes devoted to Allah (*lillāh*) and commits wholeheartedly to returning to his Lord. This leads to a transformation, where the disciple becomes a guiding figure within his family, shifting from being guided by his parents to being followed by them. This change occurs because the disciple has dedicated himself to the spiritual inheritor of the Prophet ﷺ, who is a member of the Prophet's esteemed *'itra*.

In a related vision, a disciple dreams of walking along a narrow, razor-sharp path and notices a mountain that initially appears in front of him but then positions itself behind him. This vision reiterates a key spiritual lesson: if the disciple prostrates before Allah ﷻ, even the mountains will follow him.

How, then, does one genuinely prostrate before Allah ﷻ? The disciple must continuously focus on the ultimate pursuit of spiritually discovering Allah ﷻ. He should constantly question the purpose of his presence in the *Zāwiya*, ideally doing so three hundred and sixty times daily.

This number, three hundred and sixty, corresponds to the number of primary blood vessels in the human body. By consciously overseeing his *nafs* at least this many times a day, the disciple will direct all his vessels toward the paramount pursuit: the knowledge of Allah ﷻ.

*

The Love for the Shaykh Is More Important Than the Vision of the Light

One who beholds the Light but does not hold love for the Shaykh neglects a fundamental principle of the faith, which is the bond with the *'itrat ahl al-bayt* (the elite of the Prophet's progeny). Imam al-Tirmidhī, in his *Sunan*, documents a hadith narrated by sayyidunā Zayd ibn al-Arqam ☙ where the Messenger of Allah ﷺ stated: "Truly, I entrust to you that which, if you hold firmly onto, will shield you from deviation after me. Understand that one of these is more significant than the other: the Book of Allah ﷻ, a rope extended from the sky to the earth, and the elite of my progeny (*'itratī ahli baytī*). They shall remain inseparable until they reunite with me at the Pool (*ḥawḍ*). Thus, take care in how you treat them after me."

An individual who receives the Light and then proclaims, "The Light has been bestowed upon me by Allah... the Shaykh is simply a conduit," and regards the Shaykh as no more than a transient figure, a tool that expires after passing on the Light, will see his Light extinguished. This reflects a lack of reverence for the legacy of the Prophet ﷺ.

For ascension to the heavens, both ropes (the Qur'ān and the *'itra*) are indispensable. Cutting one makes the ascent unattainable.

And Let it be known to humanity that the day there are no longer descendants of the Prophet's family ﷺ on Earth, there will cease to be the Book, the Qur'ān.

*

The True Enemies of the Shaykh

A disciple sent a dream to Sidi Shaykh, in which the latter was in Sudan, gathering Sudanese Karkaris and urging them to fight his enemies. The same disciple shares a second dream: he was at home when a heartfelt intuition informed him that the Prophet ﷺ would visit him. He prepared by dressing in his finest clothes. However, as he descended, he heard that the Prophet ﷺ was arriving with his companions, and upon opening the door, he was confronted by a black dog.

In the context of the first dream, it's important to understand that the true adversaries of the Shaykh are the forces of darkness (*al-ẓulumāt*). This darkness has manifested itself in many humans and *jinn*. The dream's message is to combat darkness by actively engaging in *daʿwa* among the Sudanese people. Essentially, *daʿwa* represents a critical battle that a disciple must wage against his own personal darknesses.

The second dream serves as a response to the first. The black dog symbolizes Satan, as conveyed in the sunna. Satan epitomizes darkness, a barrier that obstructs one's understanding and connection with the Prophet ﷺ.

Herein lies the potency of Satan's influence. He poses here in the dream as a hindrance between the disciple and the vision of the Prophet ﷺ. The real enemy is not the one who inflicts injustices upon you; in fact, such individuals inadvertently benefit you as they imbue you with Light. The genuine enemies are the forces of darkness, for they instill tyranny (*ṭāghūt*) within the soul (*nafs*) and divert a disciple from the path of Light to that of darkness.

*

Everything Originates from the Shaykh

Then, this disciple tells us that before starting his wird, he tries to visualize the blessed image of Sidi Shaykh to lend sanctity to the practice.

It is not necessary for the disciple to recall the image of his Shaykh before commencing his *dhikr*. Rather, he should instill in his heart the belief that everything he perceives originates from the heart of his Shaykh. Thus, the disciple directs his focus directly toward his origin, which is the Shaykh. One must continually remind oneself that the source of all luminous manifestations (*tajalliyāt*) is none other than the Shaykh. The disciple should understand that everything he experiences emanates from this blessed heart. He who views things in this manner will find his spiritual journey shortened.

We teach the disciple to always return the trust to its rightful owners. Sayyidunā al-'Alawī ﷺ, the Shaykh of our Shaykh, would advise his disciples: "if you pray alone, intend that I am your imam, and your prayer will count as if it were in a congregational setting."

This guidance stemmed from the fact that the disciples of that time had a genuine spiritual connection with their Shaykh. This does not mean that the disciple should distance himself from the community. Quite the contrary, it is obligatory for him to attend the mosque upon hearing the call to prayer, *adhān*, to pray in congregation. Nevertheless, today's disciples have yet to attain the level of *taslīm* (submission) necessary to follow in the footsteps of Sidi Aḥmad al-'Alawī ﷺ.

*

Beware of Asking Allah for
the Station (*maqām*) of a *Walī* (saint)

A disciple sent a message to Sidi Shaykh, informing him that one of his ancestors was a walī. This disciple had repeatedly prayed in the mausoleum of his grandfather, seeking the same station (maqām) that his ancestor held during his life. Following these prayers, trials began to afflict him. After one such visit to his grandfather's mausoleum, his condition drastically changed. He started to feel the weight of mountains on his shoulders and his soul seemed to burn. He suffered so intensely that he began crying like a child. Entering the Tariqa alleviated this condition somewhat, but it still persists. What is the solution to this ordeal?

It is advised not to seek the stations of other *awliyā'* (plural of *walī*) during one's spiritual journey, as the paths they traversed to reach these stations remain unknown to you. You do not comprehend the burdens they shouldered to achieve their *maqām*. Allah ﷻ prepared them for such challenges; they could endure these afflictions and trials without a word of complaint, keeping their struggles private. They were shaped to bear immense burdens. Allah ﷻ granted this disciple what he fervently desired; now he is obliged to endure it, due to his relentless pursuit.

Indeed, the disciple must comprehend that he is distant, weak, and not worthy of any *maqām*. He should persistently seek forgiveness and the favor of Allah ﷻ and pray for annihilation (*fanā'*) in Allah's gentleness (*lutf*) and love. It is unwise to request a *maqām*. Some aspire to the *maqām* of Sidi Abu al-Ḥassan al-Shādhili ﷺ. It is important for these individuals to be aware that he faced expulsion from Morocco, Tunisia, Algeria, and Libya, endured significant hardships, and ultimately died from poisoning. And yet, you aspire to that *maqām*?! Are you prepared to bear the burden of these trials?! Consistently implore Allah ﷻ to bestow upon us annihilation in His beauty (*jamāl*) and contentment; this way, the disciple will navigate with grace, *lutf*. Those who desire majesty (*jallāl*) often fail to recognize their own insignificance and weakness.

The Prophet ﷺ said that when a believer is stung, he ﷺ feels it twice as intensely. The Prophet ﷺ shares the suffering of each believer, out of mercy for the community and to illustrate our relative insignificance compared to Him ﷻ.

Therefore, it is advised that the disciple who sent this question return to the mausoleum where he prayed and to earnestly beseech Allah ﷻ to relieve him of the *maqām* he had requested.

*

Beware of Falling into Incarnation (*ḥulūl*) and Unity (*ittiḥād*)

Another disciple reports that when using public transport, he perceives people not as distinct individuals but as a unified entity.

This perception is nonsensical because the physical eye discerns distinct units. It sees Muhammad, ʿAlī, Fatima, among others, indicating that it remains within the realms of dispersion and plurality. A person who, through this eye, perceives only a singular unit is indeed veering towards the doctrines of incarnation and unity. Such an individual mistakenly conflates Allah ﷻ with His creation, a deviation from which we seek protection from Allah ﷻ.

Allah ﷻ never amalgamates with His creation, for the Real Existent cannot be confined and contained within the perishable. Those who acknowledge the Divine Unity only perceive His blessed Light, transcending and originating the perishable forms. These individuals are exceedingly rare. Conversely, a disciple who deems that the Divine mingles with the creation may gravitate towards Buddhism, from which may Allah ﷻ safeguard us.

In the Qur'ān, Allah ﷻ describes humanity as a plurality ("**O people!**"), whereas the soul (*nafs*) is singular. Allah ﷻ created us from one *nafs* ("**We created you from a single *nafs***") and from this *nafs*, He created its pairs. The one who attains the first *nafs*, namely the *nafs* of the Prophet ﷺ is in the realm of the first unity/unit.

To illustrate: imagine walking through a marketplace, yet perceiving only the Light, nothing else. Those who reside in this spiritual station (*maqām*) would find it challenging to leave their homes, as they perceive solely Light upon Light. They no longer see the mundane (*dunyawī*); they exist beyond this physical world. Such individuals, for example, could inadvertently cause traffic accidents.

Similarly, consider the experience of sayyidunā Mūsā ﷺ who lost consciousness when the Light began to erase the images around him.

*

The Birth of a Daughter Is Always Good News

This same disciple informed Sidi Shaykh that his wife is expecting a daughter and asked him to suggest a name.

The finest female names are those given by the Shaykh to his five daughters, as well as the names of the Prophet's daughters ﷺ. The names of Sidi Shaykh's daughters are Wi'ām, Aya, Ala, Wala, and Ḥirā. The names of the Prophet's daughters ﷺ are Fatima, Umm Kulthum, Zaynab, and Ruqayya.

Allah ﷻ bestows glad tidings upon the father graced with the birth of a daughter, or whose first child is a daughter, reflecting His profound mercy. A daughter remains a steadfast companion to her parents, offering support and prayers for them during their lifetime and beyond.

Additionally, a father who successfully arranges his daughter's marriage is promised a place in paradise. Such a birth is a cause for celebration. The one who first welcomes a daughter into his family is rewarded with plentiful *rizq* (provision), in contrast to sons who may bring challenges, trials, and weariness.

Session VII
November 14, 2020

*

Understanding the Nature of Light Is a Good Sign

A disciple mentions that he is beginning to discern the Light of Allah ﷻ, the Light of the Prophet ﷺ, and the Light of the walī.

In this spiritual journey, the seeker navigates through these three Lights. Initially, he immerses himself in the Light of the Shaykh, then progresses to the Light of the Prophet ﷺ and ultimately experiences the Light of Allah ﷻ. Understanding that the Light traverses these three stages signifies the disciple's growing comprehension of the spiritual path.

*

Always Return to the Source

In a vision, a disciple sees the name of the Prophet ﷺ alongside another unfamiliar name.

When encountering proper names during a vision, the disciple should focus on the most familiar ones. For instance, if presented with names like Ibrahīm, Mūsā, ʿĪsa ﷺ along with the name of the Prophet, sayyidunā Muhammad ﷺ, he should always gravitate towards the Prophet's name ﷺ. He should direct his attention to the most eminent prophet, in this case, the Messenger of Allah, Muhammad ﷺ.

If the Prophet's name were absent, the disciple should turn towards the name of Ibrahīm, and so forth. For a deeper understanding of the manifestation, the disciple should always orient himself towards the most eminent source.

*

The Manifestation of the *Qabḍa Nūrāniyya* (Luminous Grasp) Illustrated by the Earth

Indeed, the earth harbors a lamp (the terrestrial core) placed by Allah ﷻ at its center. Digging into the earth reveals this lamp (*miṣbāḥ*). The layers beyond this core can be seen as representing the Glass (*zujāja*). These layers give rise to what is found on the surface, on earth, representing the Niche (*mishkāt*), the last veil (the thinnest and most delicate).

In reality, the surface of the Earth is merely a shadow compared to its other components. Our "existence" might be likened to each of us being a point within the niche, having an image solely because of the light from the lamp, reflected onto an atom of the Glass (*dharra mina al-zujāja*).

By grasping this atom on the Glass, the disciple folds his dimensions and time and reads his book. Returning to his original atom in the Glass, he comprehends *zaman balā* (the time of pre-eternity), when he bore witness to his Lord's oneness. Yet, the profoundest truth he might realize is the non-existence of his being, that his existence is akin to a mere dot.

Despite this realization, it is alarming that the disciple might focus on his body and *nafs*, attributing sanctity to their existence.

*

Changing Destiny?

Know, O disciple, that if Allah ﷻ has destined you to face a trial, nothing can stop it. Supplications can soften it and make it more bearable. However, those who do not arm themselves with *dhikr* and supplications will invariably face trials with full intensity.

*

All Answers for the Believers' Questions Are Found in the Word of Allah

A woman sees herself in a dream, ill and seeking medicine. Someone comes to her, hands her the Qur'ān, and says, "Read it."

The Qur'ān is a source of healing for believers (*al-mu'minīn*). Allah ﷻ states in *Sūra* al-Isrāʾ, verse 82: **"We send down in the Qur'ān that which is a healing and a mercy for the believers. Yet, this only increases the loss of the unjust."**

This promise does not apply to everyone but only to those who have reached the level of faith (*al-īmān*), as Allah ﷻ, in this verse, addresses the *mu'minīn*, not merely Muslims. One who seeks healing will find it in the Qur'ān, for everything lies within the word of Allah ﷻ: every science the disciple wishes to uncover, every solution he needs for his problems, and every means to achieve wealth is in this Book. It encompasses all knowledge for education, becoming a scientist, and even understanding history.

In essence, the divine word holds an answer to everything. The sole requirement for the seeker is *īmān*. Without it, he cannot expect to attain anything previously mentioned. It is also a misconception to think that these answers are accessible through intellect, as if one could understand the Qur'ān simply by using intelligence.

Understanding does not require intelligence; the fundamental prerequisite is a pure heart.

*

What Is *Jalāl*, Truly?

The concept of *jalāl* is not what the disciple believes it to be. *Jalāl* is not just the trials we experience in the transient world. Knowing that you are transient, that the world you inhabit is transient, and that the transient essentially does not exist, in truth, these trials are non-existent. They are merely illusions. This is the reality. Therefore, where is the trial? Where is the *jalāl*?

Here, in this world, there is no *jalāl*.

True *jalāl* is to be consumed by the Light. This Light must burn the disciple so profoundly that he no longer feels his own soul. He who truly experiences this state will come to understand the real *jamāl*.

Consider Sayyidunā Ibrāhīm ﷺ as an example. Without his annihilation (*fanā'*) in Allah ﷻ he would not have willingly entered the fire his people had prepared for him. If he had viewed these trials as *jalāl*, he would have avoided them.

His *fanā'* in Allah ﷻ was so complete that when he was cast into the fire, the fire itself was consumed by the annihilation and *jalāl* of Ibrāhīm ﷺ. This fire had become a mere atom in the reality of Ibrāhīm ﷺ. Since Love is *jalāl*, its essence is like a fire. Ibrāhīm became the true embodiment of the fire of love. The physical fire did nothing but extinguish itself in the fire of Ibrāhīm ﷺ.

This very fire is the source of all *jamāl* found in the malakūt of Allah ﷻ. It is the Light through which celestial manifestations are revealed to the disciple during his *dhikr*.

True *jalāl* is being struck by the Light and losing all sense of existence. All the trials the disciple faces in this life, as previously stated and reiterated, are transient. And an illusion can be neither *jalāl* nor *jamāl*.

*

What Is the Difference Between a Prophet, a Messenger, and a *Walī*?

A messenger or emissary (*rasūl*) is someone who brings a divine message for the people of his era. This message contains new laws from Allah ﷻ, known as *sharī'a*. From this message, the messenger reveals the stations of religion: *islām*, *īmān* (faith), and *iḥsān* (perfection). The *sharī'a* may be directed either towards a specific people or towards all humanity.

A prophet (*nabiy*) is one who reminds people of the message of the preceding messenger, addressing those who have deviated from the right path. He restores them to order, yet always operates under the auspices of the messenger who came before him.

Wilāya, unlike the other two, is directed towards a specific group of people who believe in the latest message of their time: the faithful (*al-mu'minūn*).

The role of a *walī* is to guide believers from the darkness of their *nafs* to the Light of the Real (*al-Ḥaqq*).

A messenger is both a *walī* and a prophet. A prophet is a *walī* but not a messenger, and a *walī* is neither a messenger nor a prophet.

*

The Confrontation Between *Risāla* (message) and *Wilāya* (sainthood) in the Story of al-Khiḍr and Mūsā

Sayyidunā al-Khiḍr was a *walī* (saint) and sayyidunā Mūsā ﷺ was a messenger. In seeking out al-Khiḍr, Mūsā ﷺ represented the Message (his exoteric knowledge, *risāla*) and obscured his own *wilāya*. Al-Khiḍr represented *wilāya* (esoteric knowledge) but was under the *sharīʿa* (religious law) of Mūsā ﷺ, under his guardianship. By visiting al-Khiḍr, Mūsā ﷺ confronted the *risāla* with *wilāya*.

Indeed, even though the *risāla* is universal, it belongs solely to the realm of *mulk*, the physical world. In contrast, *wilāya*, which is exclusive, pertains to the *jabarūtī* order, involving complete annihilation. Therefore, the *risāla* cannot encompass *wilāya*. Since *wilāya* is the source of *risāla*, it means that *risāla* is merely the final trace of *wilāya*. When al-Khiḍr guided Mūsā صلى الله عليه وسلم through the secret, he manifested this complete annihilation in the *mulk*. Mūsā صلى الله عليه وسلم was overwhelmed and astonished but did not deny or turn against al-Khiḍr.

His exoteric concerns were legitimate, but had he known how to trace what he witnessed back to the source, he would have realized that al-Khiḍr's actions were aligned with *sharī'a*. Witnessing a child's killing is not easy. In apparent *sharī'a*, it is strictly forbidden to kill a child, even if the child commits a crime.

Al-Khiḍr's act of slaughtering the child, though difficult to accept, did not lead Mūsā صلى الله عليه وسلم to renounce his *wilāya*. Indeed, *wilāya* originates from the *jabarūt* and represents total annihilation, not adhering to the rules and laws of plurality. Therefore, it cannot be conflated with the *risāla*, which belongs to the *mulkī* world and is limited to forms (*ṣuwar*) and appearances (*maẓāhir*). This is for instance unlike prophecy, which is *malakūtī* and exists between the physical world and total annihilation.

Al-Khiḍr did not reveal the secrets of prophecy indiscriminately. He revealed them to Mūsā صلى الله عليه وسلم. Revealing secrets to the unworthy constitutes an act of disbelief. Mūsā صلى الله عليه وسلم harbored *wilāya* in his heart. Those who think al-Khiḍr committed disbelief by revealing these secrets to Mūsā صلى الله عليه وسلم should be reassured; Mūsā صلى الله عليه وسلم was capable of accepting these secrets.

A disciple discerning these three Lights in his heart: that of Allah ﷻ, of the Prophet ﷺ, and of the *walī*, is beginning to understand the path. However, he will only truly comprehend these Lights upon reaching the *alif al-muqaddar*, specifically by studying the *risāla* at this station. Then, the disciple realizes that the *risāla* does not surpass the *mulk*, that prophecy is the *malakūt* of the Most Merciful, and understands the origins of the secrets received by the prophets. The true secrets of *wilāya* only begin after the disciple journeys through the seven readings, as *wilāya* is a total annihilation in the dot, achieved through complete submission (*taslīm*).

These secrets of *taslīm*, *al-musāllamāt*, are transmitted heart to heart, not spoken or written.

Ultimately, the seven readings speak of Prophecy (*nubuwwa*). *Wilāya* comes after this journey through the seventy secrets. Journeying in the Supreme Name, Allah, is not *wilāya*. During these sessions, we discuss only the *risāla* and *nubuwwa*. Yet, we sometimes give the disciple a glimpse of *wilāya*, revealing signs such as, "The name Allah is not pronounced, yet you pronounce it," or "The Name you read and write is written without script and read without letters."

We never speak directly of *wilāya*, as the disciple progresses through stages, passing through the *risāla* and *nubuwwa*. *Wilāya*, being *jabarūtīyya* and supreme, requires the disciple to completely annihilate his *nafs* (ego).

Next, the disciple must navigate the *musālamāt* (wordless sciences), heart to heart, to taste the secret of *wilāya*. The Light of *wilāya*, unconfined, oversees all Light, whether the Light of prophecy or that of the message. The other two Lights always challenge the Light of *wilāya*, as they are confined and cannot perceive beyond their limits, despite originating from *wilāya*. Man often opposes what he does not understand. The most profound Light the disciple studies on this journey is the Light of the Supreme Prophecy (*al-naba' al-'aẓīm*). When he himself becomes Light upon Light, he will have fulfilled the Supreme Prophecy. Yet, even at this station, he has not entered *wilāya*. His journey continues until his heart, limbs, and every aspect of his being become Light, including his skin, muscles, nerves, and veins. However, even then, he has not yet penetrated the secrets of *wilāya*. Entry into these secrets occurs only after surpassing the seventieth secret.

The essence of the Light of *wilāya* is supreme. All secrets acquired by the disciple are merely a bridge laid by the *walī* to guide him to the *alif*. Upon reaching the *alif* and declaring "I" (*anā*), the *walī* inverts his journey making him enter the dot of the *risāla*, instead of that of the *musāllamāt*. If the disciple enters with his *nafs* (ego) unburnt, he is doomed.

The true servant, the knower by Allah (*al-'ārif billāh*) extinguishes himself in the Essence (*al-dhāt*) through supererogatory acts. He is indifferent to both hellfire and paradise. Continuing to worship Allah ﷻ for His Essence, even when destined for the fire, is the mark of a true servant (*'abd*). This path is followed purely out of love, as only love propels one forward in such a journey.

If a disciple's attributes align with those of the *walī*, he will take on the Attributes of the Most Merciful (*al-Raḥmān*). Through this, the disciple learns the meaning of the Attributes, a realization that occurs only in the supreme prophecy (*al-naba' al-ʿaẓīm*). These Attributes are referenced in the hadith of the *walī*, where Allah ﷻ says: "I will become his Vision, his Hearing, his Hand."

However, the *walī* transcends this stage, which pertains to the Supreme Prophecy. *Wilāya* exists at a higher degree: "When he calls upon Me, I grant what he wishes, and when he seeks refuge, I provide it." When the *walī* desires something, it materializes through mere intention.

When he wishes to extinguish passions, he does so effortlessly. This is his "refuge with Allah." The passions flee from the *walī*, as hellfire disintegrates in the face of a realized believer's Light.

Who can wage war against a man of such stature? No one can contend with one who has achieved extinction in Allah ﷻ. This person has surpassed the *maqām* (station) of Light upon Light, as this station is prophetic. The *walī* reaches the *maqām*: "And sanctify for Me the Light."

One who enters the *alif*, recognizing his non-existence, will gain access to *wilāya*. One who, at this *maqām*, claims "I" (*anā*) and sanctifies his existence, becomes akin to Iblīs.

Session VIII
November 23, 2020

*

**This World Is Merely Ruins,
Therefore Do not Attach Yourself to It**

*The session begins with a disciple's recounting of a vision.
As he prostrates, before him he sees houses in ruins.*

Understand that Allah ﷻ is showing this disciple the true essence of this world. Indeed, this transient world is nothing but ruins. These ruins represent the obstacles that hinder disciples from attaining the presence of Allah ﷻ owing to their attachment to these worldly hindrances. For example, disciples may contemplate owning a house or starting a family. Prioritizing such worldly matters and taking them to heart is the actual impediment on the disciple's spiritual journey.

During *dhikr* (remembrance of Allah ﷻ), the disciple ought to intend in his heart to embrace all the entire influx of Light contained within. He should also focus solely on the *dhikr* of Allah ﷻ and the annihilation into

111

His Light. Furthermore, in his *dhikr*, the disciple should implore Allah ﷻ to shorten his path, enabling him to reach His presence more swiftly.

If a disciple encounters visions such as ruined houses while in a state of *dhikr* with closed eyes, he is advised to open his eyes and divert his attention from these visions. He should resume his *dhikr* solely to behold the Light.

*

The Star Is Light: The *Nafs* Is Darkness

Subsequently, a disciple reports envisioning the Light of the radiant star dimming, turning darker, and the star itself becoming shadowy.

Be aware that the radiant star is Light upon Light. It is considerably improper to describe it as this disciple has. The truth is, the *nafs* (ego) is what is dark, having eclipsed this radiant Star.

Imagine this: The disciple's heart is so enveloped in darkness that it veils the Light of the Star. Essentially, the disciple is turning away from the Star, and this is why he perceives no Light. Indeed, every goodness originates from Allah ﷻ and every evil emanates from one's own *nafs*, as depicted in the Qur'ān.

Allah ﷻ declares in *Sūra* al-Nisā' (The Women), verse 79: **"Whatever good comes to you is from Allah; and whatever misfortune befalls you is from yourself. We** have sent you as a Messenger to the people, and Allah is sufficient as a Witness."

Reflect on the vision of the prostrating disciple: the one who witnessed debris and ruins. His specific attachment to the *dunyā* (worldly life) weakens his perception of the Light. Some approach the Shaykh to take *bayʿa* (pledge of allegiance) not with the intention of seeking knowledge of Allah ﷻ but rather to improve their material conditions and attain a comfortable life. Allah ﷻ simply reveals to them the truth of the *dunyā* they ardently desire: It is nothing but debris and ruins, nothing else.

*

The Lower World (*dunyā*) Is a Defilement

A disciple sees in a dream that he is cleaning toilets.

When a disciple sees toilets in a dream, he should know that they symbolize the *dunyā* (worldly life).

When Sayyidunā Ādam ﷺ ate from the tree, the impurity generated within him could not remain in Paradise. This necessitated his descent to Earth. Consequently, Earth became the repository for the impurity originating from what Sayyidunā Ādam ﷺ ingested. Thus, this impurity ultimately returned to its source.

To enrich the soil, farmers utilize manure composed of animal fecal waste. Humans then consume plants and fruits grown from this earth, nourished by these wastes.

Sahl Ibn Sa'd al-Sā'idī ﷺ reports that the Messenger of Allah ﷺ said: "If this lower world had even the value of a fly's wing in the sight of Allah, He would not grant a disbeliever even a sip of water."

Since the fly feeds on filth, it serves as a reminder for the disciple to strive to overcome his attachment to the *dunyā*. He must relinquish it, for by doing so, the *dunyā* will naturally depart from his heart.

*

Allah's Light Is Everywhere with the Disciple, but the Disciple Is not Always with Allah

A disciple, while in the toilet, experiences a vision with both closed and open eyes, where the Name of Allah ﷺ appears written in Arabic and illuminated.

This vision transcends space and time, for it is the Light of Allah ﷺ that gave rise to space and time. Allah ﷺ is present with His servants in every location, be it a mosque or a bar. The challenge lies in our ability to remain conscious of His presence. Seeing the Light in such a setting as a toilet is thus not unusual.

Al-Shushtarī ﷺ, renowned as a profound knower of Allah ﷺ, claimed to see Allah ﷺ in everyone and every-thing, including Jews, Zoroastrians, and even boars. His deep connection with Allah ﷺ allowed him to perceive the divine everywhere.

The more a disciple beholds the Name of Allah ﷻ, the closer he aligns with the Supreme Name. The more he perceives the attributes of Allah ﷻ, the deeper his understanding of the vision of the Light and its four examples becomes. A disciple who journeys through the Attributes will gain a more profound understanding than one who focuses solely on the Name. He will savor the Name more throughout his path and attain a greater comprehension of the Essence of his Lord.

*

Accepting Things as They Are

In a dream, a disciple finds himself with Sidi Shaykh, who is eating salad. The disciple suggests washing the salad again to protect Sidi Shaykh from encountering worms. However, Sidi Shaykh declines, remarking, "No, otherwise the religion will exhaust you."

As stated in a hadith, if a man attempts to adhere to the entire religion, it will exhaust him; indeed, it will overcome him. A disciple should not overly concern himself with others, particularly his children, wife, and immediate circle. He must learn to accept things as they are.

*

Learning to Converse with the Lord

Is it permissible to recite the Qur'ān in prostration and to repeat a word from a verse as dhikr?

According to *sharī'a*, reciting the Qur'ān in prostration is forbidden. It is also not allowed to repeat a word from a Qur'ānic verse, as each word possesses an established Light. Repeating it without proper knowledge is akin to taking medicine without understanding the dosage, which can become hazardous.

The only acceptable reason to repeat a verse is in efforts to comprehend it. However, repeating it for personal benefit without adequate knowledge or permission is strictly prohibited.

For those who wish to repeat a Qur'ānic verse, they can envisage a dialogue with Allah ﷻ in their minds, given that the Qur'ān is His Word. For instance, if a Qur'ānic verse tells the reader, "The believers will enter paradise," the reader should respond, "O Allah, please include me among them." If another verse mentions, "The disbelievers will go to hell," the reader should then say, "O Allah, ensure that I am not among those individuals." Following this method the disciple will gain a deeper understanding of the Word of Allah ﷻ.

*

Permission for *Siyāḥa* Is Mandatory, as Is Starting it in a Group

A disciple from Bangladesh seeks Sidi Shaykh's approval to go on a spiritual trip (siyāḥa).

A disciple is allowed to undertake *siyāḥa* only with the Shaykh's consent. At the outset, a disciple must not embark on this journey alone, and the group's size for *siyāḥa* should be an odd number.

In the initial stages of the spiritual journey, it is especially difficult to proceed alone. A disciple will not receive spiritual benefits if he ventures out alone at the beginning of his journey. It is after acquiring experience in group *siyāḥa*, learning patience alongside his brothers, that he might consider solitary ventures. Participating in group *siyāḥa* often reveals interpersonal challenges, through which patience is fostered. This guideline is universal, even for a disciple from Ethiopia accustomed to undertaking solo *siyāḥa* on foot over extensive distances.

The founding principle of *siyāḥa* teaches more than just patience. Experiences like the absence of food, drink, and shelter, along with other challenging situations, provide profound teachings for the disciple.

*

The Patched Garment Reflects the Lamp

A disciple noticed brothers wearing patched garments and inquired about their significance.

The patched garment is akin to the lamp. The lamp symbolizes the initial state of Light. Through its colors, it represents the reflection of this primal Light. It is the unity (*al-jam'*) that appeared in differentiation (*al-farq*).

*

How to Visualize the Light?

A sister, who took the bay'a over two months ago, has yet to see the Light. She has an autistic child and requested Sidi Shaykh to pray for her to see the Light and to find a spiritual remedy for her son's condition.

Those who embark on the path do so via the gateway of *istighfār* (seeking forgiveness). This is the daily *dhikr* (remembrance) to be performed consistently. Moreover, even if a disciple accesses our teachings, he won't grasp them if he hasn't seen the Light. Regrettably, without spiritual flow from the Shaykh, the disciple will be unable to understand even a small aspect of the journey. Indeed, it is the Light that imparts understanding and knowledge to the disciple.

A person who fails to see the Light post-commitment must isolate himself and persist in his *dhikr* until he beholds it. He must be diligent in adhering to the conventions of *dhikr*. He should maintain his *dhikr* sessions as on the day of his *bay'a*. On that day, he sat in a state of ablution, donned attire in line with the sunna, and sat cross-legged. At that moment, his heart was imbued with profound reverence; he was in awe of Allah ﷻ, with his heart in prostration, practicing *istighfār* to discover Allah's Light.

Entering the path requires performing two *wirds*: one after *ṣalāt al-ṣubḥ* and another after *ṣalāt al-maghrib*. The disciple should also not neglect *qiyām al-layl*: waking up an hour and a half before *ṣalāt al-fajr*, and spending an hour in *istighfār* with the previously described sanctity.

*

Trials as a Sign of Divine Love

Regarding the ill child, the sister should endure her trial patiently. Every trial from Allah ﷻ is a mark of His love for His servant. al-Tirmidhī, in his Sunnan, cites Sayyidunā Muṣ'ab ibn Sa'd ibn al-Waqqās ؓ who narrated from his father about a man asking: "O Messenger of Allah ﷺ, who faces the most severe trials?" He replied, "The prophets, then their closest followers, and so on. A person is tried in accordance with the level of his faith;

if his faith is firm, his trials are harder; if he is lax in his faith, his trials are according to his faith. A servant will continuously face trials until he walks on the earth free of sin (like the angels)."

In another narration by Ibn Mājah, Sayyidunā Anas ibn Mālik ﷺ relates that the Prophet ﷺ stated: "The magnitude of the reward corresponds to the severity of the trial. When Allah, Exalted be He, loves a group of people, He tests them. Whoever accepts [Allah's decree] earns Allah's satisfaction, and whoever resents it incurs Allah's wrath."

We are unable to cure this child as he is in a different country. His healing lies with his doctor. The Shaykh's role is to annihilate the *nufūs* (souls) to bring them into the presence and knowledge of Allah ﷺ. The disciple must, at least once in his life, sit with his Lord to know Him and invoke Him, not to seek worldly gains such as children, wealth, health, etc.

It's noteworthy that we perceive autism not as modern science does, but as a malady of the soul. This may surprise some, but we see it as an affliction of the soul. Indeed, the knowledge of the people of Allah (*ahlu l-llāh*) ﷺ differs markedly from modern medicine. If we find a spiritual avenue, we can potentially heal this child.

*

The *Qibla* in the Maghreb

This disciple also sees in a dream a sun rising.

The interpretation of the sunrise symbolizes the *qibla*. Indeed, we prostrate in the direction of the sunrise. When this disciple took the *bay'a*, she understood that the *qibla* is the Shaykh. Therefore, she must stop wandering aimlessly, she must listen to what We tell her, and she must cease all actions that distance her from our guidance. This is how she will see this sun in a vision while awake.

*

Patched Clothing: The *Sanad* (evidence) of Sayyidunā 'Umar

A Syrian disciple reports dreaming of Karkari disciples wearing patched garments. They were circling around the Light of the Throne, receiving a spiritual flow. Then, they invited him to wear the patched garment.

The patched garment is the most attacked foundation in the Tariqa. Many people, including some scholars, deny wearing this garment, which was not chosen and worn arbitrarily. We have a chain of transmission that goes back to the Prophet ﷺ through Sayyidunā 'Umar ؓ. Among all the companions, it was he who wore it, and the people of Allah ﷻ have always dressed this way. Those who deny this garment do so either out of ignorance or jealousy.

*

The only Authentic *Khulwa* Today

Another foundation of the Tariqa concerns the spiritual retreat, *khulwa*. The only Tariqa where an aspirant to Allah ﷻ can have a true *khulwa* is the Tariqa Karkariya. Elsewhere, he will never reap its fruits. Worse, those who claim to conduct *khulwa* for their disciples today, without obviously having any *idhn* (permission), literally drive them mad.

*

Sanad of the *Subḥa* in the Qur'ān

We are also asked about the *idhn* of the *subḥa* (prayer beads). This *idhn* indeed comes from the Holy Qur'ān where Allah ﷻ says in *Sūra* Āl-'Imrān, verse 191: **"Our Lord, You have not created this in vain! Glory to You (*subḥānak*), save us from the torment of the fire."**

This is the *subḥa*; it is what will save you from the fires of hell. The *walī* has brought these verses down from the *malakūt* (heavenly realm) to the *mulk* (physical realm) and derived the *subḥa* as a foundational practice for the path, which the Karkari disciple wears around his neck.

*

The Shaykh Will not Instruct a Disciple to Adhere to the Foundations of the Path; This Responsibility Falls on the Disciple Himself

Sayyidunā Ādam ﷺ was the first to don patched garments when he descended to Earth. In Paradise, after consuming the forbidden fruit and being commanded by Allah ﷻ to descend, he arrived on Earth clothed in leaves from the tree of the fruit he had eaten.

The Syrian disciple, who was not wearing patched garments, observed that only other disciples were receiving blessings by forming a *ḥadra* circle around the Throne. He recognized that without this attire, he too would miss out on the blessings of this Light. This realization prompted him to consider that perhaps it was time for him to don the garment. At this stage of the journey, it is quite regrettable to admit such a realization.

We have indeed authored a comprehensive book, which Sidi Suhayl (Adrien Zapata) has translated into French. May Allah ﷻ protect him. This book outlines the seven foundational principles of our path. These principles are also available on the Tariqa's French website, a platform where Sidi Suhayl has made significant contributions.

Every disciple entering the path is expected to wear patched clothing. The Shaykh does not individually remind each disciple of this obligation. It is incumbent upon the disciple to familiarize himself with the Tariqa's foundations and to implement them in his journey.

If we specifically instruct a disciple to wear patched clothing and he fails to comply, he thereby breaches his commitment, which could disastrously impact his spiritual progression. The Shaykh's silence on this matter is a form of mercy. Instead, we present the seven fundamentals of the Tariqa, leaving it to the disciple to apply them as best as he can.

A disciple can also undertake *khulwa* alone at home. If he lacks the *idhn* to invoke the Supreme Name, he may perform it through *istighfār*. The *khulwa* led by the Shaykh serves as an assessment to gauge the disciples' spiritual state.

*

Shame Befalls One who Asks the Prophet to Purify His Heart

A disciple expressed to Sidi Shaykh his anticipation for the Prophet ﷺ to enter his heart and cleanse it of its idols.

The Prophet ﷺ does not enter hearts that harbor idols. It is the Shaykh's role to rid the heart of impurities. The Shaykh acts as the custodian of the Owner's House, the house being the heart and its Owner, the Prophet ﷺ. Asking the Prophet ﷺ to cleanse one's heart demonstrates a severe lack of decorum and diminishes the stature of our Prophet ﷺ. The disciple is responsible for cleansing his own impurities. When the Prophet ﷺ enters a disciple's heart, it is solely to bestow Knowledge. While the disciple may seek Allah's help in purifying his heart, requesting the Prophet ﷺ to undertake this task is highly inappropriate.

Al-Ḥākim ﷺ relates in his book *al-Mustadrak*, as narrated by Jābir bin 'Abd Allāh ﷺ from the Prophet ﷺ: "I am the City of Knowledge and 'Alī is its Gate; whoever desires knowledge must enter through this Gate."

Historically, it was Sayyidunā 'Alī ﷺ who purified the place of the Prophet ﷺ. He perfumed and prepared it before the Messenger of Allah ﷺ arrived to impart His Knowledge. He ﷺ is the Embodiment of Knowledge, and He imparts it only in a pure heart.

*

Denounce Yourself Before Becoming
the Mockery of All

In the initial stages of their spiritual journey, disciples often find themselves overwhelmed by arrogance, self-admiration, and greed. These vices are attributes of *Shayṭān* and are deeply embedded in the individual, making them hard to eliminate.

A disciple who has been consistently devout in mosque attendance may feel superior to others. Such a disciple will journey through hardship. Conversely, one who acknowledges personal flaws, such as indulging in wine or associating with women, tends to view himself as inferior to others. He becomes oblivious to his *nafs* (ego). When granted the Light, such a disciple advances swiftly, driven by a deep aversion to his *nafs*, free from greed, arrogance, and self-satisfaction. His flaws are evident; a known drinker, for instance, has no grounds for preaching. When seeking *bay'a*, his sole pursuit is repentance (*tawba*), not miracles. His aim is solely to gain Allah's approval. Those who struggle most in their spiritual progress are often those who have memorized the Qur'ān, consider themselves from a noble lineage, or hold academic qualifications. These disciples tend to recognize the good in themselves while seeing the bad in others. It is extremely challenging to make them understand that they might be more tainted than their brethren.

Wearing a patched garment is advised for such individuals to help eliminate arrogance from their hearts. Those who fear public opinion over Allah ﷻ and who are unable to follow the founding principles of the path due to fear of criticism, essentially fear creation over the Creator.

On your path, confess to your Shaykh if you are arrogant, greedy, or morally corrupt before Allah ﷻ reveals you to the world, turning you into a laughingstock of the very creation you feared.

Recall the companion of the Prophet ﷺ who couldn't refrain from drinking wine. Whenever he succumbed, he would present himself to the Prophet ﷺ, admit his actions, and accept the prescribed *sharīʿa* punishment. This occurred several times. On one occasion, after repeating the offense, a companion suggested to the Prophet ﷺ that the offender might be a hypocrite and offered to execute him, perceiving the repeated actions as insulting.

The Messenger of Allah ﷺ responded: "No, he genuinely loves Allah and His Messenger." This was evident as the companion was unafraid to consistently expose his faults before the Prophet ﷺ seeking Allah's pleasure. He was not enslaved by others' opinions but was devoted to his Lord.

Believers should aspire to such sincerity. This level of honesty with Allah ﷻ is lofty and challenging to attain. Believers of this nature quickly draw near to Allah ﷻ as they see only Him, even amidst their sins.

*

Focus on Your *Nafs*

A sister visualized during dhikr four men carrying the Kaʿba, with Sidi Shaykh above it.

These are the four Poles of the Seal (*khatm*) of the *awliyā'*, [i.e. Sidi Shaykh may Allah sanctify his secret].

Indeed, each *khatm* has four poles. They are called the pillars of *wilāya* (*arkān al-wilāya*). We fear revealing them to others because we are concerned about attributes like arrogance for them and greed for others. Furthermore, what is the benefit of knowing the poles of the Tariqa, when the most important task, knowing one's *nafs*, remains unaccomplished?

The disciple should always try to see his own *nafs* and not that of others. He should strive to uncover his own maladies and try to treat them. This is invariably better than focusing on the maladies of others. The Prophet ﷺ said, upon returning from a battle: "We have returned from the lesser *jihād* (*al-jihād al-aṣghar*) to the greater *jihād* (*al-jihād al-akbar*)." When asked, "What is the greater *jihād*?" He ﷺ replied: "The struggle against oneself."

*

The *Mīm* Studies the Heart Through the Colors of the Forty Stations of the *Nafs*

This woman sees in her vision the letter mīm (م) in red light.

This disciple must strive to extinguish himself in this red light, which corresponds to the *nafs* that incites to evil (*nafs al-ammāra*). The color in which the Light appears is merely a sign describing the station of the *nafs*. This is always preferable to seeing darkness.

The *mīm* is one of the letters in the name of the Prophet ﷺ and this letter is written twice in His Name ﷺ. The *mīm* represents the name of the Prophet ﷺ in this lower transient world. The name Aḥmad, written with an *alif*, represents the name of the Prophet ﷺ in the heavens. The *mīm* also symbolizes the forty degrees of the *nafs* as its numerological indice in the Arabic tradition is forty. One who surpasses the forty degrees of the *nafs* becomes a *muḥaqqiq*. The *muḥaqqiq* is one who has unified esoteric and exoteric knowledge. This station is called the *Aḥmadī* station.

When the Messenger of Allah ﷺ appeared in the physical world, His *nafs* was *mīm*, and He ﷺ was called "Muhammad." Thus, we say: "Muhammad" with a *mīm* on earth, and "Aḥmad" with an *alif* in the heavens.

The name "Allah" ends with the letter *hā'*. In writing, the *hā'* represents a circle. The *mīm* is also written similarly. The end of the name "Allah" is the beginning of the name Muhammad. It's as if the *mīm* and the *hā'* represent the same thing. That's why we say there is no intermediary between Allah ﷻ and Muhammad ﷺ.

However, the *alif* is transcendent and is represented by a line that is neither confined nor rounded.

One who possesses the knowledge of the *mīm* will study the heart through the colors of the forty stations of the *nafs*. These colors are studied in the *hā' al-huwiyya* (the *hā'* of Identity) because it's in the *hā'* that one studies the Names of Allah ﷻ. These Names all have a reflection of Light in the Glass (*zujāja*), each manifested as a color. For example, violet refers to the name *al-Walī*, blue to *al-Muḥīṭ* (the All Encompassing), orange to *al-Malik* (the Sovereign King).

In the *hā' al-huwiyya* are the ninety-nine divine names. The hundredth name is the secret of all these names. They all derive their flow from this Name, and this Name also infuses all the Names. It's called the Supreme Hidden Name, which appeared through the name "Allah" in this physical world, but its truth and essence remain always hidden.

He who bears this Name is the Seal of his time. He flows into all the divine Names and is referred to in the hadith in *Ṣaḥīḥ* of Imam al-Bukhārī ﷽. Sayyidunā Abū Hurayrah ﷺ reports that the Prophet ﷺ said: "Allah created Ādam in His image," and in another hadith: "Allah created Ādam in the image of the Most Merciful (*al-Raḥmān*)."

*

The Shaykh as the Hundredth Name

The sister also sees in her vision the Name "Allah," and in the hā', she sees the image of the Shaykh.

In fact, this confirms what we have just explained. The Shaykh represents the hundredth name; he is the key to the Supreme Name (*ism Allah al-aʿẓam*), and that is why the disciple sees him at the center of the *hā'*. He is, simply put, the Vicegerent of Allah ﷻ (*khalīfatu Allāh*).

Session IX
November 30, 2020

*

**Everything That Veils You
from the Light Originates from Your *Nafs***

A disciple recounts having had two consecutive dreams. In the first dream, he finds himself in front of the full moon, but there is a very thin veil between him and the moon. He notices something written in Arabic on it, which he cannot read. The following night, he sees the same moon with the same veil; however, this time he manages to read the inscription but has no memory of what was written upon waking. Sidi Shaykh asks the disciple, "How do you see the Light?" The disciple replies that when he is spiritually present, he sees a star, from which halos of Light emanate.

Sidi Shaykh explains that between this disciple and the moon lies the subtle veil of the *nafs*, and any veil that separates a human being from his Lord originates from his own *nafs*. Thus, for the disciple to access the vision of the full moon, he must maintain a state of continuous *dhikr* (remembrance), focusing his sole objective in life on the Light. He must perceive it in everything, before everything, and after everything. Anything that stands between the seeker and the Light must be emphatically eliminated.

*

Tasting the Divine Essence Through the Attribute

The Qur'ān is an attribute (*ṣifa*) of Allah ﷻ, as it is the Word of Allah ﷻ. The Light is also an attribute.

The disciple can know the Essence of Allah ﷻ through the attribute of speech because God's Word has never been separate from Him. Similarly, with the Light. The disciple will immerse himself in this Light, which is an attribute, thereby tasting the Divine Essence.

*

Contemplating a Single Formula to Know Him

Allah ﷻ has provided a formula through which we can bridge the distances to know Him. Allah ﷻ says in *Sūra Āl 'Imrān*, verses 190 and 191: **"Those who reflect on the creation of the heavens and the earth."**

Allah ﷻ has thus presented us with the tool for attaining His knowledge: the heavens and the earth. These can be compared to the *subḥa* (rosary), which also serves as a tool leading to the knowledge of Allah ﷻ. Yet the heavens and the earth are Light, and it is the disciple's responsibility to meditate on their creation, constantly engaged in continuous *dhikr*.

*

Meditation Through *Dhikr* Transmitted by the *Wāsiṭa*

Reflecting on our existence today, we realize that even perishable things have become superior to human beings, despite humans being the Viceregents (*khalīfa*) of Allah ﷻ in the *mulk* realm. Indeed, every perishable thing performs the *tasbīḥ* (remembrance) of Allah ﷻ and praises Him. Human beings, however, have strayed and distanced themselves from this practice. Thus, the disciple must consistently engage in the morning and evening *dhikr*, the *tasbīḥ* instructed during the *bayʻa* (initiatic pledge) commitment. Between these, he should always be in *istighfār* and never abandon it. Only then can he become the Viceregent pleasing to Allah ﷻ.

On the Day of Judgment, the disciple cannot claim before his Lord, 'Why did I not possess knowledge?' His Shaykh has given him everything through this *wird*, which emanates directly from Allah ﷻ. This *wird*, containing all the light of the heavens and the earth, is often ignored and not held sacred by many. Therefore, one should never resort to another *dhikr*. This *wird*, though brief, is immensely replete with Light. The heavens and the earth themselves exist by the Light of this *wird*; without it, they might never have come into being. Additionally, this *wird*, that is imbued with the Light of the heavens and the earth, is illuminated by the Blessed Tree (*ash-shajara al-mubāraka*), and thus grants access to extraordinary spiritual elevation.

If We grant the disciple the *idhn* (permission) to invoke this *wird*, and yet he turns to other *awrād* (plural of *wird*), other spiritual paths, or other Shaykhs, he essentially turns his back on Us. Such a disciple will never achieve true knowledge.

*

The *Wāsiṭa* as Either a Veil or a Gateway

Allah ﷻ created the heavens, the earth, and all they contain. These elements are tools for attaining His knowledge. When humans descended to earth, they fell into *ghafla* (heedlessness) and began searching within this creation for ways to reach Allah ﷻ. They discovered the *wāsiṭa*, the intermediary between themselves and knowledge, namely the *walī*. It is he who endowed them with the Light necessary to comprehend the surrounding creation—the heavens and the earth—and to attain knowledge.

Instead of utilizing this *wāsiṭa* to know Allah ﷻ, humans transformed it into a barrier. It became a veil for them.

Some disciples started to seek from the Shaykh things other than the knowledge of Allah ﷻ, such as *ruqya* (spiritual healing), employment, or marriage. Consequently, they are being tested by the Shaykh for the deviation of their intentions. Modern disciples resemble Sayyidunā Nūḥ's son, who saw his father ﷺ not as a vehicle to attain knowledge of Allah ﷻ but rather as an obstacle.

Similarly, Pharaoh, instead of recognizing Sayyidunā Mūsā ﷺ as a conduit to Truth, rejected him, turning him into a veil between himself and the truth. Pharaoh, indeed, failed to perceive that Mūsā ﷺ was the intermediary through whom he could have attained the knowledge of Allah ﷻ.

*

Begin Meditating on the Heavens Before the Earth

Allah ﷻ says in the Qur'ān, in *Sūra* al-Nūr, verse 24: **"Allah is the Light of the heavens and the earth."** To discover and attain knowledge of Allah ﷻ the disciple must first meditate on the Light of the heavens (*samāwāt*), as Allah ﷻ begins by mentioning the heavens, not the earth.

The Light of the heavens is closer to Allah ﷻ. Those who meditate on the creation of celestial bodies, stars, or lunar abodes, as well as all who meditate on celestial phenomena, are engaging in the first step toward the knowledge of the Truth.

Only after meditating on the Light of the heavens should the disciple turn to the terrestrial Light. Why not begin with the earth? Although humans have always inhabited the earth and are continually in contact with Allah's creation, they have not achieved true knowledge of Him.

In practice, everything on earth acts as a veil between the servant and the knowledge of their Lord. The heavens, unknown to the disciple, are like a hidden, elevated treasure. In the common human imagination, the heavens are perceived as lofty. As long as the disciple has not experienced the proximity of Allah ﷻ on earth, even though He is closer to him than his own *nafs* (self), he should meditate on the Light of the heavens. By following this path, he will bridge distances and quickly come to know Allah ﷻ. Hence, we consistently advise the disciples: "Stop thinking of your children, your money, or your spouses, etc." This advice is not to imply abandonment, but rather to highlight the potential danger posed by one's immediate environment, to which one may have already become enslaved.

*

Why Does Man Desire Wealth and Worldly Goods?

These originate from the Earth. The children and spouses we love are made of clay, as described in the Holy Qur'ān. And clay comes from the earth. This earth then becomes the greatest obstacle to accessing the knowledge of Allah ﷻ.

The Shaykh emphasizes that when the disciple came to take the *bayʿa*, he was given the Light of the heavens. Consequently, the first thing he received was his elevation to the first heaven. Despite this, the disciple reverted to his earthly desires, for which he should feel ashamed. The first heaven enables him to observe stars, galaxies, constellations, and other celestial bodies. Yet, the disciple is drawn back by the gravitational pull of the earth. His pursuit of hidden treasures underground, professional or familial achievements, and the like, represents the true challenge in his journey towards Truth! The disciple came to ascend in the knowledge of his Lord, but he cannot abandon his earthly desires. This lower world attracts him like a magnet, so much so that we fear for him on the Day of Judgment.

*

How to Escape Earthly Attraction?

The *wird* (litany) we have given to the disciple serves as a *burāq* (celestial mount), enabling the disciple to escape this earthly attraction. Thus, teach your children to gaze toward the sky. Educate them in contemplation and the exploration of the heavens. Say to them, "Observe the sky and reflect on how Allah ﷻ created it!" "Notice its vastness, limitless and endless." "Contemplate its beauty." They will learn to spiritually ascend in the immensity of the sky and, crucially, avoid being drawn down by the earth. Indeed, when we gaze at the heavens, we perceive them as infinite and beyond confinement, in contrast to the sense of limitation we experience on Earth.

This is why, in the supplications from the sunna for a deceased person, we pray for the horizons of their grave to be expanded infinitely. Wherever they look, they should see a horizon without bounds.

*

Surpassing the Seven Heavens to Understand Earth

In his spiritual journey, the disciple cannot return to the earth until he has gained knowledge of the seven heavens. Only after completing this stage can he then reflect on the creation of the earth. At this juncture, he can apply the same contemplative process he used for understanding the heavens to the earth, as his capacity for reflection will have broadened. He will possess the ability to be unbounded within confinement (*taqyīd*). Consequently, he will become a trace (*athar*) of the Message and the manifestation of the *sharī'a*. Although living in the *mulk* (physical realm), he will interact with those around him as if he were in the *malakūt* (heavenly realm). Thus, he becomes *malakūtī* in the *mulk*, celestial within the terrestrial world. If the disciple has not yet acquired knowledge of the seven heavens, he cannot claim to truly know himself. Knowledge of the *nafs* (self) is attained through understanding the seven heavens, which, in reality, reside within him. Therefore, when reading the Qur'ān, wherever his gaze falls, he will connect it to what he learned in the divine presence while in the heavens. He will recite verses 190 to 192 of *Sūra Āl 'Imrān*: **O Lord, You have not created this in vain, Praise be to You, protect us from the punishment of the fire of hell (...).**

Consequently, a seeker cannot fully grasp the Qur'ān in its essence until he reaches the seventh heaven. To understand it, he must first understand his *nafs*.

Consider the examples of the Prophets ﷺ, who are in the heavens, to grasp this concept. The most notable example is Sayyidunā Ādam ﷺ, who resides in the first heaven. In this realm, he acquired the knowledge of the Names. Yet, he left Paradise and descended to Earth. Therefore, he did not completely know his *nafs* in this heaven. This is why he had to descend to earth to continue his journey there.

Similarly, 'Īsā ﷺ, Yūsuf ﷺ, and Ibrāhīm ﷺ did not achieve full knowledge of their *nafs*; the only one who transcended the seven heavens to reach the ultimate height is the Prophet Muhammad ﷺ, the sole individual to have completely understood his *nafs*.

The Shaykh, acting as an educator, offers the seeker a rope to ascend into the heavens. By adhering to his guidance, he can rise from one heaven to the next. He can only claim to truly know his *nafs* after ascending this rope.

*

Reading the Qur'ān in the Heavens for Understanding

The Qur'ān is not of earthly origin, but celestial. It is akin to the rain descending from the sky, rejuvenating the earth. In a hadith, The Prophet ﷺ said: "I leave you two weighty things: the Book of Allah ﷻ and my progeny (*'itra*). The Book of Allah ﷻ is like a rope stretched from the sky to the earth, and my progeny are my family." Thus, a disciple can only truly comprehend the Qur'ān by reading it in the heavens.

In the Qur'ān, Allah ﷻ describes not only the scholars of the Children of Israel when He likens them to a donkey carrying books, but He also refers to all those who consider themselves scholars yet lack Divine Light. Allah ﷻ says in *Sūra* al-Jumu'a, verse 5: **"Those who were entrusted with the Torah, but failed to uphold it, are like a donkey carrying volumes of books. Wretched is the example of the people who deny the verses of Allah. And Allah does not guide the unjust people."** The donkey, naturally an earthbound animal, has its head and gaze constantly downcast, towards the ground. Similarly, one devoid of the Light is comparable to the donkey, his vision never transcending the earthly realm, even if he bears the Qur'ān.

This is also why the interpretations of the Qur'ān by a *walī* emanate from the heavens, while the understandings and interpretations of scholars remain grounded in earthly knowledge.

The disciple must not overlook the seven rings/niches manifested in the vision, for it is by this rope that he will ascend and attach himself in the heavens. He will climb the ladder of knowledge that the Shaykh has laid out.

He starts with the first reading in the first heaven through the lineage of Sayyidunā Ādam ﷺ, then progresses to the second heaven to grasp how the Qur'ān was revealed to Sayyiduna 'Īsa ﷺ and so on, until reaching the seventh heaven. Through the Mercy of Allah ﷻ and the love of the Prophet ﷺ the disciple will acquire the seven readings.

After these profound realizations, the seeker returns to earth to reflect on all that is there, but now through the Earth's Light.

Nonetheless, even upon embarking on this spiritual path, the disciple continues to yearn for earthly pleasures, indicating he has yet to grasp the necessity of transcending them. He should not even entertain these thoughts. His quest must lie in the heavens: this must be his sole focus.

He may pursue them once he has folded the seven heavens into his heart, a feat far from simple. Yet, this remains the only path to acquiring divine knowledge.

*

How to Ascend Through the Heavens?

In Arabic, the word *ruqiy* refers to elevation. The more a disciple ascends through the heavens, the more he escapes the confines of this earth. The people of Allah ﷻ were once blessed by the inhabitants of the heavens, though not on earth. One who ascends through the heavens will thus be blessed by its inhabitants but ignored or even fiercely attacked by the inhabitants of the earth, except for those whom Allah ﷻ has chosen as his companions. Therefore, a disciple journeying through the heavens will have the inhabitants of the heavens as his companions.

The first step towards ascension is *istighfār* (seeking forgiveness).

Al-Bukhārī reports in his *Ṣaḥīḥ* that the Prophet ﷺ said: "Every night, when the last third of the night arrives, our Lord, blessed and exalted, descends to the lowest heaven and says: 'Is there anyone to call upon Me so that I may respond to his invocation? Is there anyone to ask of Me so that I may grant his request? Is there anyone seeking My forgiveness so that I may forgive him?'"

Despite this, disciples are so attracted to this earth that they always seek recourse in the *sharīʿa* to do as they wish. They are completely absorbed by the veil that is the earth, especially during *dhikr*. This is why the best advice the Shaykh gives his disciples to try to disconnect them from this earthly attraction is to imagine themselves as dead (mimicking the state of sleep) during *dhikr*, for one who is dead can no longer even operate his thoughts.

*

The Only One to Achieve Total Knowledge
of His *Nafs* Is Our Prophet Muhammad

We have previously explained that the only human being to have achieved total knowledge of his *nafs* (self) is our Prophet Muhammad ﷺ because he surpassed the seven heavens. He fulfilled himself in the seven readings of the Supreme Name. We have understood that it is crucial to meditate on the creation of the heavens and the earth, starting with understanding the Celestial Light, then superimposing this understanding onto the Light of the Earth, and thus descending into the *mulk* (worldly realm) to become the perfect embodiment of the divine Message. Accomplishing this will induce prophetic behavior towards the images (*ṣuwar*) of the earthly world.

So, what is the proof of the Prophet's realization in the seven readings of the Name?

The proof is his right of intercession on the Day of Judgment on behalf of his community. He ﷺ will be the only Prophet able to intercede. According to authentic hadiths, on that dreadful day, all Muslims will be in a state of panic, fleeing from one Prophet ﷺ to another to spare them the ordeal of that day. They will all respond: "We cannot intercede on your behalf."

The only one who will not shy away from their request will be the Prophet Muhammad ﷺ. He will respond affirmatively, as described in the blessed sunna.

Indeed, He ﷺ is the only Prophet who has succeeded in fully realizing himself. However, for the sake of decorum, it should never be said that any prophet did not realize himself. Yet, in the ultimate truth and through *wilāya* (sainthood), He is the only Prophet who achieved perfect realization. He is the only one to have fulfilled himself without an iota of imperfection. This is precisely why He obtained the supreme intercession.

*

Elevation Through the Heart, Not the Intellect

In our Tariqa, the seeker ascends from heaven to heaven, transitioning from one marvel to the next. Understandably, those who dwell in the heavens differ from those who inhabit the earth. The Karkari disciple will no longer be preoccupied with earthly concerns, as his mind will be constantly connected to and absorbed by celestial horizons. Each niche (celestial sphere) is a station where the seeker must pause to understand the secrets of that heaven. The journey culminates with the Star, the brightly shining Celestial Body, the Moon, and finally, the eternal Sun. It is disheartening when a disciple observes these niches of Light but remains unsatisfied because his *nafs* (ego) craves, for instance, to see the image of a man dressed in white in the vision! This becomes the ultimate expectation for many! Indeed, man was created with a *nāṣiya* (spiritual forelock) steeped in falsehood and error.

However, the part that elevates a person is not his intellect but his heart, for it is in the heart that the descent of divine knowledge occurs. This is confirmed by a hadith reported by al-Tirmidhi: the Prophet ﷺ said, "When Allah created Ādam, He touched his back, and from it fell all his descendants until the Day of Judgment. He then placed a mark of Light between the eyes of every one of them..."

This beam of light exists between the eyes of all humans, yet the knowledge of Allah ﷻ is not present there; it contains neither niche, lamp, nor celestial body. The Qur'ān reveals in *Sūra* al-Baqara, verse 257, the source of the luminous flow of knowledge: **"Allah is the *Walī* of the believers: He brings them out of darknesses into the Light."**

The verse describes the Light of the *Walī* (saint), intended for believers, not all Muslims. Those who have not yet transcended the station of *al-islām* cannot claim access to this Light. In a saying by sayyidunā Ibn 'Abbās ؓ, faith (*īmān*) is described as a Light that Allah ﷻ casts into the heart of the believer.

It is this Light that enables servants to attain the knowledge of Allah ﷻ and to discover and know their *nafs*, ascending through the heavens, sky after sky, reading after reading.

*

The Door to the Light Is Unique: Islam;
While All Other Doors Originate from the Dajjāl

This Light, as previously mentioned, is described by Allah ﷻ, in *Sūra* al-Nūr, verse 35: **Allah is the Light of the heavens and the earth. The exemplification of His light is like a niche within which is a lamp, The lamp is within glass, the glass as if it were a resplendent star, Lit from [the oil of] a blessed olive tree, Neither of the east nor of the west, Whose oil would almost glow even if untouched by fire. Light upon light. Allah guides to His light whom He wills. And Allah presents examples for the people, and Allah is Knowing of all things.**

This Light is specific to Muslims and is not granted to all humanity. Neither Christians, Jews, Buddhists, nor followers of any religion outside of Islam have access to it. Those who claim otherwise are in utter misguidance, engulfed in complete illusion. Anyone who believes non-Muslims can access the Light has a flawed and deceitful *nāṣiya*, with *nāṣiya* here referring to the intellect.

Understand that the true purpose of *sujūd* (prostration) is to purify the intellect from lies and errors.

The disciple, continually in a state of purification, whether through ablutions for his outward reality or by purifying his intellect (*nāṣiya*) through prostration, knows with certainty that only the white path of the Prophet ﷺ (*al-maḥajja al-bayẓā'*) leads to this Light. He reaches such a level of discernment that he would tell his

Shaykh: "The disbelievers are but dust; they are non-existent." The Shaykh will remind him to maintain proper conduct towards Allah's creation, saying: "They are human beings created by Allah ﷻ."

Unfortunately, many of today's youth, and even some believers, influenced by contemporary ideas, fall into the misguidance of the Antichrist (Dajjāl), trying to include non-believers among the bearers of knowledge of Allah ﷻ.

From the sunna of our Prophet ﷺ, we know that the Antichrist has the word *kāfir* (disbeliever) written on his forehead, binding him to those who lack belief. These people are thus his progeny.

Imam al-Bukhārī and Imam Muslim, in their *Ṣaḥīḥ*, cite Sayyidunā Anas ibn Mālik ﷺ reporting the Prophet ﷺ saying: "There has not been a prophet who did not warn his community against the one-eyed liar. Indeed, he is one-eyed, and your Lord is not. It is written between his eyes: *kāfir* [disbeliever]."

To purify one's intellect from such disbelief, one must be in *sujūd* constantly and daily. This is why the people of Allah ﷻ cherish long hours of prostration, seeking the purification of the *nāṣiya*.

The story of the Children of Israel's deviation, especially during the incident of the Golden Calf crafted by al-Sāmirī in the absence of the Prophet Mūsā عليه السلام, who had left them in the care of his brother Hārūn عليه السلام to uphold monotheism (*tawḥīd*), is a vivid illustration. When Mūsā عليه السلام returned and saw what had transpired, he was taken aback by the misguidance that had unfolded under his brother's supervision. In a moment of profound significance, he grasped Hārūn ﷽ by the beard and the forehead, the *nāṣiya*, the site of prostration to Allah.

The manner in which Mūsā ﷽ held Hārūn ﷽ was deeply symbolic, particularly focusing on the *nāṣiya*, which misled the Children of Israel. In this prophetic story (*ḥaḍra*), Mūsā ﷽ epitomized the supreme prostration. Holding his brother at the very spot of *sujūd*, Mūsā ﷽ questioned the lapse that led them to bow before anything other than Allah ﷻ.

Understand that the light from the nāṣiya lacks the four Qur'ānic depictions of Divine Light, namely the Niche, the Lamp, the Glass, and the Shining Planet. It is through the nāṣiya that humans are often led astray. In contrast, these four Qur'ānic examples ﷺ guide believers heavenward, illuminating the essence of Divine Lordship.

*

Al-Khalīfa al-Maknūn (The Hidden Viceregent)

One must relinquish his *nafs* to fulfill the role of becoming the Viceregent of Allah on earth and in the heavens. The aim is to ascend and savor the knowledge of the Real through His Names, His Attributes, and His Essence.

Afterwards, the disciple will descend from the heavens back to the earthly world to fulfill his role as an accomplished Viceregent. He will be clothed in the garment of

Lordship, yet will bear the appearance of an ordinary servant. Endowed with the Attributes of the Most Merciful, his spirit and soul will also be imbued with mercy. At this station, the disciple will carry within himself the Hidden Supreme Name (*al-ism al-aʿzam al-maknūn*).

He will bear this Name because his truth and reality will be concealed in the earthly realm. Earth's inhabitants won't recognize him; only those in the heavens will. This Name, The Stamp, which is the sign of accomplishment, can only be understood through the disciple's ascension into the heavens. Hence, it remains inaccessible to those in the worldly realm.

In the story of Sayyidunā Mūsā ﷺ and Sayyidunā al-Khiḍr ﷺ in *Sūra* al-Kahf, verse 65, Allah ﷻ says: **"They found there one of Our servants, upon whom We had bestowed Our mercy, and to whom We had imparted a [special] knowledge from Ourselves."** This Mercy and knowledge emanate from a higher plane, specifically from heaven, not from earth. Allah ﷻ in *Sūra* Ṭā-Hā, verse 114, also says: **"Exalted be Allah, the True King! Do not hasten with [the recitation of] the Qur'ān before its revelation to you is completed, and say: 'My Lord, increase me in knowledge!'"** Thus, it is crucial to continually make this supplication throughout one's life, thereby perpetually maintaining one's ascent and growth in divine knowledge.

*

Who Will Be Saved in this Journey to Allah?

The companion Abu Saʿīd ﷺ narrates that the Prophet ﷺ said: "I am about to be called [by Allah] and I will respond. I leave you amongst you the two weighty matters, hold firmly to them: The Book of Allah and the elite of my descendants (ʿitra). The Book of Allah is like a rope stretched from heaven to the earth, and my descendants are my family. Indeed, The Subtle, The Informed, has informed me that they will not be separated until they come to me at the pool [on the Day of Judgement]. Therefore, be mindful of how you will treat them after my departure."

This hadith demonstrates the importance Muslims should place on the bearer of the Light. They should cling to it with the hope of being saved. As for those who do not believe in it, they will not be saved.

In reality, despite his inability to fully comprehend the events unfolding around him, the Karkari disciple, who claims to see stars in his vision and ascends into the heavens, resides in this magnificent celestial world. He is the one liberated from earthly attraction.

Deniers will surely say: "What are you talking about! This is nonsense!" Unfortunately, these people will be deprived of the knowledge of Allah ﷻ. They will live and die with this mindset.

The disciple of this luminous path wonders why the people of Allah ﷻ led solitary lives with few companions?

Secretly, they formed bonds with the inhabitants of the Heavens, and from then on, had no need for earthly companionship or knowledge.

For those who have not joined the Light of Allah ﷻ they have remained with the appearances of the path and forgotten its essence, as taught in *Sūra* al-Ḥadīd, verses 12 and 13: **"On that day, you will see the believing men and women with their Light streaming before them and to their right; [it will be said]: 'Today, good news for you: gardens beneath which rivers flow, to abide therein forever.' That is the immense success. On that day, the hypocrites, both men and women, will say to those who believed: 'Wait for us, let us have some of your Light.' It will be said: 'Go back behind you (to *dunya*) and seek light.' Then a wall will be put up between them, with a gate in it. Inside it will be mercy, and on the outside, punishment."**

This verse reveals that on that day, the believers will see the hidden side (*bāṭin*) of this wall, which represents the niche (*mishkāt*) of Mercy. In contrast, the hypocrites will behold the outward (*ẓāhir*) side, essentially a gateway to Hell. Thus, it becomes clear why, in the end times, during the *fitna* (trial) of the Antichrist, his paradise will in fact be Hell, and his Hell will be paradise.

*

What Is the Solution for Allah's Servants to Be Protected?

The Prophet ﷺ teaches us as reported in *Ṣaḥīḥ Muslim* on the authority of Sayyidunā Abū al-Dardā' ؓ: "Whoever memorizes ten verses from the beginning of *Sūra* al-Kahf, The Cave, will be protected from the Antichrist (al-Dajjāl)." And in another version: "... from the end of *Sūra* al-Kahf."

It's about returning to The Cave... As if the Prophet ﷺ is telling us that we need to isolate ourselves, withdraw from this worldly life, from all its earthly preoccupations, and try to elevate ourselves in the knowledge of the Real.

This knowledge is in the heavens, and to ascend to the heavens, one must become a celestial spirit, and above all, protect the secret of Allah ﷻ. One must emulate the attributes of the dog of the cave, who protects the secrets of Allah and knows how to be humble and faithful to the Bearer of the Secret. By accumulating these characteristics, the disciple will become a supreme truth and annihilate himself in the Niche of al-Muṣṭafa ﷺ. And this door is the only way to be rescued by the Lord.

Higher education will bring nothing to its bearers on the Day of Judgment, for success lies in the knowledge of the One who created us, not in the science that confined intellect extrapolates and extracts from creation.

To attain this knowledge, one must join the school of al-Muṣṭafa ﷺ which studies the Creator through His creation and this, by the secret of the Light. If earthly sciences were meant to save people, then disbelievers, Buddhists, and Christians would already have their places in paradise. Yet we know that they will be punished in hell. Allah ﷻ says in *Sūra Āl-'Imrān*, verse 85: **"And whoever seeks a religion other than Islam, it will not be accepted from him, and in the Hereafter, he will be among the losers."**

All the prophets have absorbed this science, which aim is to lead the servant to truly prostrate to the Creator. And each prophet is in prostration in the celestial station where Allah ﷻ has placed him, through the fulfillment of this supplication: "O Allah, grant us prostration under the shade of Your Throne." This means that the shade of Allah's Throne extends from the seventh heaven to the first heaven. Our Prophet Muhammad ﷺ achieved complete realization through the Supreme Prostration! In *Ṣaḥīḥ al-Bukhārī* and *Muslim*, after the refusal of all the prophets consulted to intercede between them and Allah ﷻ during that difficult day, people will go to our holy Prophet ﷺ and say, "O Muhammad ﷺ! You are the Messenger of Allah and the seal of the Prophets! Moreover, Allah has forgiven your past and future sins. Do you not see what state we are in? Intercede for us with your Lord." The Prophet ﷺ replied, "I will then go under the Throne and fall in prostration before my Lord. Then, Allah will inspire me with phrases of glorification and beautiful praise that He has never inspired in any being before me."

The goal of the Karkari in the path is to reach this prostration by invoking Allah ﷻ with the same supplications that the Prophets and Messengers used, hoping that Allah ﷻ will be Merciful to him.

Remember that in pre-eternity, Allah ﷻ created us in the heavens. He bequeathed the earth and its goods to us to live for a specific time and then to return to our original essence, which is Light. However, we have strayed because of our *nafs* and the environment in which we live. That's why the disciple's circle will constantly accuse him of being a *dajjāl* (liar) as soon as he begins to understand the truth of his existence.

*

Followers of Falsehood and People of Truth

Sidi Shaykh spoke regarding these slanderers: he who lacks a principle cannot embody it. To grasp truth, one must be both truthful and merciful. He who fails to embody these virtues will label others as liars. Indeed, the root of falsehood is a lack of mercy. Such an individual will thus slander the Karkaris with accusations that, in truth, only reflect his own character. The disciples merely act as the mirror reflecting his own image. For these people, truth does not extend beyond the mundane, revolving around bodily desires and material concerns, which is why their discussions are limited to economic crises and governmental and political fluctuations. In contrast, the people of Allah ﷻ dwell in eternal happiness, as they are unburdened by the world's concerns, its sicknesses, or its populace. Their physical bodies are on this earth, but their spirits reside with the denizens of the heavens, in the prophetic gatherings (*ḥaḍra*).

The people of Allah ﷻ have ceded this earth to those misled souls who chose to inherit its tribulations. The true believers, however, have adhered strictly to the teachings of the Prophet ﷺ. Consequently, they have inherited the Book of Allah ﷻ and the family of His Prophet ﷺ.

Session X
December 5, 2020

*

Henna, a *Sunna* of the Prophet

The session begins with a dream shared by a disciple. She recounts seeing herself among family members, sending prayers upon the Prophet ﷺ until a man dressed in white appears and asks her, "Do you have a story with the prayer upon the Prophet?" She answers, "Yes." Then, another man appears, radiant and clad in white and black garments, and tells her, "Sidi Shaykh is in the next room." Entering, she finds Sidi Shaykh with a disciple; despite not being Moroccan or the Shaykh's daughter in reality, in the dream, this disciple is perceived as her daughter. The disciple who was with Sidi asks the dreamer, "May I apply henna to you?" With her permission, the disciple takes her left hand and begins replicating the palm lines of her right hand onto it.

Henna is a sunna of the Prophet ﷺ. Seeing this sunna in a dream is a positive sign. Henna is the only dye the Prophet ﷺ permitted for his companions and his *umma*. He ﷺ allowed men to use henna on their beards to cover their white hair; any other color or dye is forbidden.

*

Disciples as the Shaykh's Children

It's important to understand that all disciples are considered part of the Shaykh's family. The hadith teaches that the people of Light do not necessarily come from the same tribe or family. This means they form a spiritual family, with the Shaykh as the father figure.

Indeed, in the interpretation of this dream, though the disciple was not Moroccan, she felt as though she was the Shaykh's daughter. The role of a Shaykh transcends geographical boundaries; a true Shaykh can have disciples from all corners of the world, and as previously mentioned, all of the Shaykh's disciples are seen as his children.

If a man claims to be a Shaykh and sorts disciples through a patriotic lens, or favors one homeland over another, it's clear that he is not genuine. The essence of being a Shaykh is measured by spirit, which, naturally, is not confined by national borders.

Consider the case of Abū Lahab, who, despite being the Prophet's paternal uncle, was certainly not among the *ahl al-bayt* due to his enmity towards the Messenger ﷺ. Conversely, Sayyidunā Salmān al-Fārisī ؓ, by virtue of his devotion to the Messenger of Allah ﷺ, was counted among the *ahl al-bayt*.

*

The Esoteric Significance of Palm Lines on both Hands

Regarding hands dyed with henna, note that in Arabic numerology, the right hand displays the number eighteen (١٨), and the left, eighty-one (٨١).

The right hand, corresponding to eighteen, leads us to 9+9=18. This reflects the nine degrees of spiritual emanation (*ilqā'*) and nine stations of receiving these nine degrees (*talaqqī*).

The eighteen of the right hand also alludes to the eighteen Apparent Divine Names. Meanwhile, the left hand contains eighty-one (٨١), representing the rest of the Hidden or Esoteric Divine Names.

Summing the numbers of both hands gives us 18+81=99, aligning with the total Divine Names mentioned in hadith. Imam al-Bukhārī reports in his *Ṣaḥīḥ*, via Sayyidunā Abū Hurayrah ؓ that the Prophet ﷺ said: "Indeed, Allah has ninety-nine names, a hundred minus one. Whoever enumerates them will enter Paradise; He is unique (*witr*) and rewards the act of enumerating these names individually."

*

Implementing What Is Understood to Reach the Secret

A disciple grasps from reading Sūra Ṭā-Hā that one must give what is most precious to the Shaykh so that in return, the latter may grant the love of the Lord, as indicated in verse 39 of the same Sūra. By making this offering, the disciple would become a representative of the wilāya and resemble Sayyidunā Mūsā.

We have selected *Sūra* Ṭā-Hā for the disciples to enable them to comprehend how to access the reading of the *lām* of passion as straightforwardly as possible. This does not imply that other *Sūras* do not inform us about the *lām* of passion, but *Sūra* Ṭā-Hā is most closely aligned with the disciples' understanding of the *lām*.

The disciple who will unlock the secrets of this *Sūra* is the one who implements the insights hidden within it. The Shaykh does not wait for the group; if one steps forward, we will welcome him. Others are required to progress to attain the rank (*maqām*) of the disciple who has unlocked the secrets of the *lām*.

*

The Disciple and the Universe

The disciple can influence the universe, just as he can be influenced by it. The one who influences the universe is he whose ultimate aim is to find and know Allah ﷻ. He becomes the core secret, the essence, or the truth of the universe. On the flip side, the one who is influenced by the universe is engaged in a constant *jihād* against his *nafs*, perpetually striving to break free from the influence of his surroundings.

Indeed, any request the disciple makes to the Shaykh, other than for the pure knowledge of Allah ﷻ such as for marriage, wealth, or employment, demonstrates that the disciple is swayed by the universe.

The Shaykh does not expect a disciple to interpret *Sūra Ṭā-Hā*, for it is the Shaykh who provides its understanding, but he does expect his disciples to put into practice what they have learned from him through this *Sūra.*

This implementation should not be in words alone but in actions that are tangible and visible. To be deserving of this *Sūra*, the disciple must emulate Sayyidunā Mūsā ﷺ. He projected his *nafs* into the *ḥaḍra* (presence of Allah ﷻ), and Allah ﷻ revealed His Truth to him; "your *nafs* is a serpent…" and then, when permitted to take it back, it transformed into a spiritual breath.

*

Ultimately, Your Efforts Stem Solely from the Grace of Allah

We must thank Allah ﷻ for taking our *nafs* (soul). We should be content with the trade we've made with Him despite the fact that, in truth, we own nothing. We do not even possess this *nafs*, for it belongs to Him. Even when a disciple believes he is exerting a great deal of effort, he must realize that this belief is illusory because it is Allah ﷻ and only He ﷻ who has bestowed this grace upon him.

A truly annihilated disciple possesses nothing and acknowledges that Allah ﷻ is the owner of all his assets. Even if he comes from a wealthy family and holds high academic degrees, he is aware that all the blessings he enjoys come from Allah ﷻ. When someone tells him, "Mā shā' Allah, you are a doctor," the disciple will respond that this is merely a blessing from Allah ﷻ and he played no part in it.

*

The Two Major Levels of Commitment to Allah

The first level involves those who have sold their *nafs*. They are the ones who will succeed in entering the *lām* of passion. *Sūra* al-Tawba, verse 111, explains this: **"Indeed, Allah has purchased from the believers their lives and their wealth in exchange for Paradise."**

The second level pertains to wealth. The fortune that a disciple believes he holds belongs, in fact, only to Allah ﷻ. Allah ﷻ is the owner of all wealth. The disciple must return what has been given to him. A seeker who fulfills these two degrees (*nafs* and wealth) will have as his provision not only the paradise of material and physical enjoyment but also the paradise of knowledge, containing the treasures of the sciences of the Names, Attributes, and Essence.

Indeed, the Shaykh loves these two categories: those who sacrifice their fortunes and those who sacrifice their *nafs*.

*

Giving Charity to the Shaykh?

The Shaykh does not accept *ṣadaqa* (charity), as it is strictly forbidden for the family of the Prophet ﷺ. However, the Shaykh does accept *hadiyya*, that is, gifts. This is also derived from the sunna of the Prophet ﷺ.

If the Shaykh decides to accept *ṣadaqa*, it is solely so that Allah ﷻ may erase the sins of the giver and to shorten his spiritual journey. That said, he will never keep it for himself or use it for personal gain. When someone comes with the intention of giving *ṣadaqa* and says they are offering a gift, we are aware of their intention, and even if we say to them: *"jazāk allahu khayr,"* we will never consume it out of fear of Allah ﷻ. For a member of *ahl al-bayt* to consume *ṣadaqa* could be more severe in the sight of Allah ﷻ than the act of fornication.

*

Preaching the Light of Allah Is the *Sunna* of the Prophets and Messengers

Sayyidunā 'Īsā ﷺ never went out to the tribes of Israel to preach the word of Allah ﷻ but sent his disciples instead.

Our beloved Prophet ﷺ was also surrounded by his companions, to whom he taught Islam. These companions would then return to their tribes to convey the teachings of the Prophet ﷺ. It is through this that the universe was transformed by the Messengers ﷺ and Prophets ﷺ.

The *walī* of Allah ﷻ follows the same sunna. He who does not propagate the Light of his Lord is not following the sunna of the Prophets. Such a person is sinning. He more closely resembles a hypocrite than a believer. If the disciple's intention is to spread this Light, Allah ﷻ will change the environment (orbit) in which the disciple lives so that it may be under his command and listen to him.

The disciple who has been imbued with the secrets of his Lord through the *walī* of Allah ﷻ must not reveal them. However, he must inform his close circle about the apparent *ni'ma* (blessing) of Allah ﷻ he has received, which is the Light.

It is only out of arrogance that one refrains from spreading this message among his close circle. He might think he is better than the Light or believe his circle is superior to this blessing. Worse still, he might try to block anyone wishing to spread the Light of Allah ﷻ. He will say: "Why are you doing this? It is the Light of Allah ﷻ not that of the Shaykh." He says this undoubtedly out of pure greed. He does not like to see others spreading this Light.

*

The Lamp, the Example Leading to Truth

In a vision, a disciple sees the Niche and the Lamp.

Allah ﷻ, speaks in the Qur'ān, in *Sūra* al-Nūr, verse 35: **Allah is the Light of the heavens and the earth. The exemplification of His light is like a niche within which is a lamp, The lamp is within glass, the glass as if it were a resplendent star, Lit from [the oil of] a blessed olive tree, Neither of the east nor of the west, Whose oil would almost glow even if untouched by fire. Light upon light. Allah guides to His light whom He wills. And Allah presents examples for the people, and Allah is Knowing of all things.**

The Light of Allah ﷻ is akin to a niche, within which sits a lamp. The Niche, mentioned at the verse's outset, has been referenced in the sunna of the Prophet ﷺ as the circles of the heavens and the earth. Afterward, the Lamp is described, leading us to understand that the Niche is defined by the Lamp. Without the Lamp, the Niche would arguably not exist. This is why the people of Allah ﷻ say that what leads to the *ḥadra* of the Prophet ﷺ is the Lamp. Without its blessed Light, neither the heavens nor the earth would be. The Light of the *mishkāt* is merely a trace of the Lamp's Light. The *mishkāt*, indeed, maps out the path leading to the Prophet ﷺ. If a disciple sees only the *mishkāt*, he glimpses the trace or shadow of knowledge without the truth of knowledge itself. One who sees the *mishkāt* must thereafter behold the Lamp. The Lamp can be identified by the three celestial examples cited in the Qur'ān, which were revealed to Sayyidunā Ibrāhīm عليه السلام.

In *Sūra* al-An'ām, verses 76 to 79, Allah ﷻ says: **"When Ibrāhīm saw a star, he exclaimed, 'This is my Lord.' ... When he saw the moon rising, he said, 'This is my Lord.' ... When the sun rose, he declared, 'This is my Lord.'"**

Thus, reflecting the Light of Prophecy, the Lamp leads to the understanding of Lordship. When a disciple is in the presence of the Lamp's example, he finds himself in the ultimate proximity to the divine. Indeed, the Prophet ﷺ stands as the ultimate veil between divinity and servitude; he who is visualizing (*yushāhidu*) the Lamp faces this ultimate truth..

*

The Dots

The truth manifests through three exemplifications: the star, the moon, and the sun. The disciple also mentioned seeing four dots in the center of the vision. These dots correspond to the physical world's diagram for the *basmala*: the dot of our mother Fāṭima al-Zahrā' ﷤, the dot of Sayyidunā ʿAlī ﷤ the dot of Sayyidunā Ḥasan ﷤, and the dot of Sayyidunā Ḥusayn ﷤.

In the *malakūt*, the *basmala* is represented by three dots–The dots of Ḥasan and Ḥusayn ﷤ converge into one.

During the Prophet's era, dots were seldom used in Arabic script. The Prophet's companions had such a deep grasp of the language that they could fully appreciate the profound impact of the Qur'ānic text without the need for dots to discern the strength of the discourse. Indeed, each of them was a dot in themselves.

The Prophet ﷺ, said: "My companions are like stars; whichever of them you follow, you will be guided." These stars are indeed the dots being referred to. It is through embodying these realities that the companions knew precisely where to place the dots in the Qur'ānic text.

*

The Language of the Secret: the Line and the Dot

To understand the lunar stations, one must first understand the language of the dot. However, this language can only be understood by mastering the language of the secret, which is deciphered not through letters but through the dot and the line.

In a hadith reported by Aḥmad, al-Nasā'ī, and al-Dārimī, on the authority of ʿAbdullah ibn Masʿūd ﷤, the Messenger of Allah ﷺ illustrated this language by drawing a line in the sand between himself and his companions. He ﷺ said: "This is the path of Allah." Then he drew lines to the right and to the left and said: "These are the trails, and on the top of each trail, there is a devil calling towards it." He then recited the Qur'ānic verse: "And indeed, this is My straight path, so follow it."

Thus, this line was drawn in the sand, which consists of countless grains. Each grain represents a dot. To reach the Prophet ﷺ along this line that he drew towards himself, the disciple must become a grain of sand, a dot. Each of the companions realized himself in a dot drawn along the same line. This line, which originates in the Blessed Essence of the Prophet ﷺ, represents the *alif*.

He who finds the dot finds the *alif*, and he who says or thinks that the *alif* is a letter has not yet understood anything. Indeed, the *alif* can only be drawn from three dots: the dot of the Message (*risāla*), the dot of sainthood (*wilāya*), and the dot of the prophecy (*nubuwwa*). If the disciple is in the *alif*, he is on the path chosen by the Prophet ﷺ. He is no longer limited by space or time, for the Prophet ﷺ is timeless.

During the journey, it is necessary to return to this dot to be continuously in the *alif*. Thus, the disciple will be among the believers who orbit around the Original Dot, which is the Shaykh, just as the companions orbited around the Prophet ﷺ. Indeed, the Dot of the Prophet ﷺ and His Blessed Family is the Dot that is the spirit of all Dot. It therefore encompasses all the secrets of the Qur'ān and, by extension, all the secrets of the universe. If the Qur'ān descended on seven letters, as cited by the Prophet ﷺ, then what can be said about the Dot that is the essence of all letters?

Through the secrets of the Qur'ān, the disciple will climb the rope that extends from the heavens to the earth. And it is through this ascent that he will attain divine knowledge and understand the Book.

Since the Qur'ān descended on seven letters, the disciple will progress through seven stages. Each stage constitutes a reading. He will move from one reading to another in this ascent along the rope that connects the Earth to the sky. In this way, he will understand the secrets of the Qur'ān. But when will he really be able to begin this ascent?

*

Understanding the Qur'ān:
Returning to the Embryonic State

As previously mentioned, the disciple must become a dot or a grain of sand to understand the secrets of the Qur'ān. However, during his time on earth, man is only comparable to a grain at the very beginning of his formation in his mother's womb, that is, at the embryonic stage.

Allah ﷻ says in *Sūra* al-ʿAlaq, verses 1 and 2: **"Read in the name of your Lord who created, who created man from a clot."**

To return to this state, the disciple must reach annihilation. Everything within him must return to the Light. At this stage, he can return to the truth of the luminous handful (*qabḍa nūrāniyya*), which is his origin, the seat of the dot from which all images draw their essence.

This is why the dot is placed over the *alif* in the Name of Allah ﷻ. It is through this dot that the understanding of the entirety of the Name is acquired.

At the beginning of the journey, the disciple finds himself very far from the dot and its elevated understanding. Allah ﷻ has facilitated the journey by making us travel through the twenty-eight letters of the Arabic language before bringing us back to the Dot.

*

One Should Never Alter the *Wird* Taken at the Commitment with the Shaykh

A female disciple sees the word "kun" (be) in Arabic in a vision and asks Sidi Shaykh if she should start invoking it.

We have given each disciple a *wird* whose content should never be changed, neither by adding to nor subtracting from it, not even by an atom. Even if the Messenger of Allah ﷺ were to come to the disciple and suggest that he take another *wird*, he should not invoke it before returning to Us.

The disciple has pledged allegiance to follow Us and to have Us interpret the signs he receives. He should therefore never precede Us or put forward the understandings that come from his *nafs*.

Moreover, the disciple has committed to this *wird* that he chants twice a day. This commitment is akin to signing a contract between the disciple and the Shaykh.

Here, the disciple only asks permission to chant the verse "*kun fa-yakūn*" (Be, and it is) because he wants to satisfy the desires of his *nafs*. He certainly does not want to attain knowledge. He is still spiritually sick. He should continue invoking the *istighfār*, which is one of the *wirds* that We give to the disciples.

By practicing it, he will obtain the continuation of the verse, namely "*fa-yakūn*" (and it is). He will continue until he engraves the entire Qur'ān in his heart.

The *wird* will give him strength, through which he will be able to uncover many things, for the Lamp will illuminate the disciple's path during his journey.

We can illustrate the way the Lamp illuminates the disciple's path with a small example: a disciple invoking his *wird* sees a *shayṭān*; this certainly does not mean that he should join him. The Lamp, in reality, illuminated his path. It turns out that this *shayṭān* is not only in his path but also in his heart. He must therefore avoid it by questioning himself.

*

The Knowledge of Allah Can only Be Transmitted Through Piety, Which Is a Light

A disciple should seek from the Shaykh only the knowledge of Allah and nothing else. Furthermore, they should understand that true knowledge is not about having numerous visions but rather the comprehension of these visions and the ability to extract the treasures they contain.

Imam al-Shāfiʿī ﷺ offers wisdom on this matter: "Knowledge is a light, and the Light of Allah ﷻ is not bestowed upon a sinner." Therefore, it is essential to guard one's tongue and chastity to learn from this Light.

Imam al-Bukhārī reports in his *Ṣaḥīḥ* that the Messenger of Allah ﷺ said: "The primary reasons people enter Hell are the mouth and the private parts." Ādam ﷺ learned the Divine Names in Paradise, which is a place devoid of sin. We teach you how to transition from sin to righteousness, to return to this paradise and learn the Divine Names.

The entire journey on the *hā'* is about *takhliya* (purification)—shedding every visceral attribute of the *nafs*. The ultimate goal of this reading is to become Light. At this precise moment, the disciple will begin to understand the sciences of the Real.

Those who learn the Qur'ān without applying its teachings are like those who have no Light yet speak of the spiritual path. Allah ﷻ mentions these individuals in *Sūra* al-Shuʿarāʾ, comparing them to criminals who have memorized the Book. Allah ﷻ says in *Sūra* al-Shu'arā', verses 199-200: **"Thus have We caused it [the Qur'ān] to penetrate the hearts of the criminals."** Allah ﷻ also describes them in *Sūra* al-Jumu'a, verse 5: **"Those who were entrusted with carrying the Torah but did not apply it are like a donkey carrying scrolls. How evil is the example of those who deny the signs of Allah. And Allah does not guide the wrongdoing people."**

The goal of studying the *hā'* is for the disciple to reach the station of purification, where they become "Light upon Light." It is at this point that true *dhikr* (remembrance) begins. Through this *dhikr*, the disciple will ascend and understand the Divine Names.

The one who reaches this station will be the fortunate purified soul, no longer distracted by anything other than Allah ﷻ. To attain this level, one must be in a continuous state of *dhikr*. Indeed, anything uttered outside the remembrance of Allah ﷻ distances the disciple from this station. This *dhikr* generates true *khushū'* (reverence), which serves as proof that the disciple has truly reached the station where *ghafla* (heedlessness) no longer exists.

*

Waken when Others Sleep

A female disciple was performing the night prayer (qiyām) but then fell asleep. In her dream, she saw two mountains before her. From behind the mountains, she heard her

Lord say, "I am your Lord. Tell your companion Youzarsif that I have indeed heard him." Upon waking at the time of the Fajr adhan, the disciple sent a message to this companion, who was in the same class as her. She informed him of the dream. He replied, "Al-hamdulillah, I spent my night weeping and imploring my Lord to give me a sign of His satisfaction. Praise be to Allah ﷻ! Now I know He is with me." The disciple then asked the Shaykh, "Does this dream concern me?"

Your Lord has given you the answer: this dream does not concern you. However, there is a lesson and a message for you to take from this dream: while you were sleeping, your companion was weeping and imploring Allah ﷻ. He was fully present with Allah ﷻ, which is why He responded to him. So, you too should stop sleeping during the time of *qiyām* and try to follow the example of your classmate.

Session XI
December 16, 2020

*

Erasing Prior Knowledge to Welcome the Light

The session began with a disciple's vision: the disciple saw in a dream three people with a mist of violet Light emanating from their heads. Sidi Shaykh came and covered their heads with a bonnet.

Allah ﷻ says in *Sūra* al-Ḥajj, verse 22: "Do you not see that to Allah prostrates whoever is in the heavens and whoever is on the earth, the sun, the moon, the stars, the mountains, the trees, the animals, and many of the people? Many are [also] deserving of punishment. And he whom Allah humiliates—there is no one to honor him. Indeed, Allah does what He wills."

The disciple should know that in his head (the upper part), Allah ﷻ has planted a blessed tree. The origin of this tree, its source and roots, are fixed in his heart, while its branches reach into the heavens. These branches form the intellect (*'aql*). Indeed, it is this intellect that exists under the shade of the heart. When a disciple enters the Tariqa Karkariya, it is imperative for him to erase all the prior knowledge accumulated before receiving the Light. He must erase it so that his vessel can be emptied and filled with the knowledge of this Light.

*

What Did the Shuyūkh Do to Their Disciples in the Past to Achieve this Foundation?

They would ask them to abandon or burn all their books! The example of Imam al-Sha'rānī, one of the greatest scholars of his time, is illustrative. He had written an impressive number of works, and his Shaykh asked him to burn them. Imam al-Ghazalī ﷺ abandoned all his works and his position at the largest Islamic school of his time, the Nizāmiyya School of Baghdad—likely the greatest university in the world at that time—to join the path of Allah ﷻ.

In our Tariqa, the approach is not quite as radical: we do not ask the disciple to erase all the knowledge acquired before the path. However, at the beginning of the journey, the disciple must strive to empty his intellect of the contents of his previous knowledge and return to them only after obtaining the secret of Allah ﷻ. At that point, he can evaluate his knowledge through the Light contained in his heart and draw from it what may assist him on his path.

Practically, the disciple may sometimes need to completely erase his previous knowledge if it is incompatible with the Light. Then, he will illuminate the knowledge that is indeed compatible with it. The knowledge he acquired before the path is comparable to pottery, and when the disciple joins the path and obtains the secret, he can breathe life into it, as his spirit has become Light.

*

The Intellect and the Spiritual Journey

Contrary to the heart, at the beginning of the journey, the intellect often hinders proper progression. It is therefore essential that the disciple disconnects it, especially at the outset during the practice of *dhikr*. At this stage, the goal is to annihilate oneself in the secret of Allah ﷻ. One should not seek to grasp the sciences of differentiation (*farq*), such as the sciences of letters. This will prolong the disciple's journey. Instead, he must gather everything into the Light to annihilate himself in the secret. Annihilation occurs in the union (al-jam'), not in the apprehension of the various sciences, which are, by nature, dispersed.

The knowledge acquired beforehand must be forgotten. The worst thing that can happen to a disciple is to continue discussing what he learned before, after receiving the secret of Allah ﷻ! The illiterate person, whose mind is void of knowledge, is in this case the most suited to benefit from the path of Allah ﷻ. His land is already ready to be tilled, with nothing planted in it. In contrast, someone who has pursued advanced studies (for example, in medicine or jurisprudence) is comparable to land that has been sown multiple times with various species. This land can no longer accommodate a new species; it is exhausted and, in agriculture, must be burned to become fertile again.

The example of Imam Ghazali perfectly illustrates this point. To progress on the path, he wiped away his vast previous knowledge, though he was the author of numerous works. He then reached the understanding of the secret of Allah ﷻ, to the extent that people still speak of him today. This is why reading the biographies of the saints, the people of Allah ﷻ, is beneficial for the disciples. It provides them with examples to follow and the motivation to implement what the path demands.

*

Emptying Oneself of the Understandings Acquired Before the Path of the Three Stations of Islam

The three men mentioned in the earlier dream represent the three *maqāms* (stations): *islām*, *īmān*, and *iḥsān*. Each man had his head covered with a bonnet by the Shaykh.

The disciple must understand that it is obligatory to forget the exoteric knowledge, such as the *Sharīʿa* (*fiqh*), that he received before the journey, and he should not involve it in what he will receive from the Shaykh.

For the second maqām, that of *īmān*, there are disciples who have studied the doctrinal proofs of Islamic belief—*ʿilm al-kalām* or *ʿilm al-ʿaqīda* (the sciences of Islamic theology). These sciences attempt to prove the truth of Islam through the intellect. These disciples must make the effort to erase all these teachings and the information they have acquired on these subjects to be able to taste the true aspect of spirituality that the people of Allah ﷻ advocate. They will then be able to experience their own journey and taste *tawḥīd* through vision.

Finally, there are disciples who have spent their lives studying Sufi books and have had access to texts describing the sciences of the people of Allah ﷻ, the history of those who have realized annihilation (*fanāʾ*), and who are in the *maqām* of *iḥsān*. These disciples must also wipe away their knowledge.

One must try to forget everything! The disciple is about to live in the pinnacle of truths! And as The Real ﷻ says in *Sūra* al-Kahf, verse 24: **"And remember your Lord when you forget."**

The disciple must forget everything he acquired before the Truth and then engage in *dhikr*.

*

Reflection (*tafakkur*) Is Dependent on Continuous *Dhikr*

One must remain in a constant state of *dhikr*, even if there are no apparent spiritual effects. Even if the disciple feels distant and does not see the *nūr* during his *dhikr*, he must keep his tongue engaged in *istighfār*, with the intention of purifying himself. When the disciple reaches a point where he can no longer abandon *dhikr*, he can then begin reflection (*tafakkur*). Continuous *dhikr* is so crucial that, at a certain stage, the disciple will be in a state of *dhikr* even during sleep.

Al-tafakkur literally means reflection or meditation. However, reflection in Islam follows a specific Qur'ānic rule. In *Sūra* Āl 'Imrān, verse 191, Allah ﷻ says: "**Those who remember Allah while standing, sitting, and lying on their sides, and reflect on the creation of the heavens and the earth, saying, 'Our Lord, You did not create this aimlessly; exalted are You [above such a thing]; then protect us from the punishment of the Fire.'**"

Thus, reflection only comes after uninterrupted *dhikr*, as highlighted in the verse: "**Those who remember Allah.**" Meditation should be focused on a single theme: the creation of the heavens and the earth. The disciple must begin by reflecting on the first cause that led to the creation of the heavens and the earth. Only towards the end of the journey can the *sālik* consider swimming or traveling (*sibāḥa*) in the *malakūt* of Allah ﷻ.

The problem with the disciple is that he wants to visit the *malakūt* directly as soon as he begins his journey. Whoever starts his journey with the *malakūt* will be overwhelmed by the images of this world, making it difficult for him to surpass them. His vessel will become saturated with images once again, and it will be much harder to empty it to later fill it with the *nūr* of Allah ﷻ. As mentioned earlier, and as has been emphasized multiple times, meditation without *dhikr* is strictly prohibited and bears no fruit. It does not grant the disciple the ability to understand the signs of Allah ﷻ.

The example of the Qurayshīs illustrates this point. They were not as foolish as people think today. They were very skilled merchants and were the best literary minds humanity had ever known. No other community in the world mastered language as well as the Qurayshīs. They had excellent intellects, but when they received the sciences of *al-Raḥmān*, they could not align their intellects with them. Practically speaking, they could not bring their intellectual prowess back to the ʿibāda of the Lord.

The people of Quraysh had developed a sharp intellect based on the apparent world, and they could not detach themselves from this construct, which they eventually began to idolize. In contrast, the Prophet ﷺ was *ummī*, meaning he outwardly did not know how to read or write. He played the role of someone who did not know, and it was then that he received knowledge from *al-ʿAlīm* ﷻ. He had the capacity to receive everything with this empty intellect. This is a supreme sign for the disciple. Indeed, clearing one's intellect allows the disciple to properly receive and understand what the Shaykh infuses in him. And this breath that the Shaykh imparts comes from *al-Raḥmān*, and its locus is, of course, the heart. As the Prophet ﷺ teaches us, access to *nubuwwa* (prophecy) and the *risāla* (messengerhood) does not come through the intellect but through direct education from the Lord ﷻ, who resides in a sound heart.

There are also those who consider themselves academic researchers in *taṣawwuf*. If their quest is not directed towards seeking a perfected Shaykh who will lead them to *maʿrifa*—which is the only true quest in Sufism—they will find themselves in the most foolish of misguidance.

Someone who, based on intellectual efforts, believes they possess any kind of knowledge is not a Sufi, even if they think that by sharing their erroneous knowledge, they are speaking about Sufism. Why would someone who claims to have spiritual knowledge approach the Shaykh and seek his guidance? The disciple should understand that the sunna of the people of Allah is to come to the *walī* as an *ummī*, just as the Prophet ﷺ demonstrated when he went to meet his Lord at Mount Ḥirāʾ. This is why the Prophet ﷺ received his education directly from the Lord, without relying on a chain of transmission from one deceased scholar to another, as the ʿulamāʾ of exoteric sciences do.

*

How Did the Prophet Receive His Knowledge?

The Prophet ﷺ received his knowledge from the school of the universes and horizons while he was guiding his flock of sheep through the mountainous regions of Mecca. This is how he received the knowledge of Allah ﷻ. The Prophet ﷺ never relied on chains of transmission.

At the beginning of the journey, the disciple cannot empty or fill his vessel until he is convinced that his Shaykh is the *walī* of Allah ﷻ. This means that when the disciple enters the tariqa, he must be certain that his Shaykh can make him taste *fanā'* in the knowledge of Allah ﷻ.

Moreover, when the disciple comes with an empty vessel, the Shaykh fills it with the four aspects of the truth. In a hadith reported by Sayyidunā al-Ḥasan ؓ the Prophet ﷺ said: "Every verse has an apparent meaning and a concealed meaning, and every letter has a limit, and at every limit, there is an ascendant meaning."

Thus, the one who comes empty will understand the Qur'ān through the four aspects mentioned above in the blessed hadith of the Prophet ﷺ. As he ascends and makes his *mi'rāj* (celestial journey), he will access the two other dimensions: that of the *mulk* (lower) and the *malakūt* (higher).

Imam al-Shāfi'ī ؓ imparted wisdom regarding this: "knowledge is *nūr* (light), and the *nūr* of Allah is not given to a sinner."

We understand, then, that the *nūr* of Allah ﷻ is not granted to those who are in sin; it is a gift (*hiba*) from Allah ﷻ and the disciple cannot attain this *hiba* through effort. Thus, all those who believe they can attain the true *'ilm* of Allah ﷻ without the *mushāhada* (vision) of the *nūr* are in sin.

*

Journeying through Colors

Let us return to the vision of the disciple who sees the color purple, corresponding to the color of the *walī*. Whoever sees this color constantly should know that his *nafs* is either in the *nafs* that is accomplished (*al-kāmila*), the *nafs* that is pleased (*al-marḍiyya*), or the *nafs* that is pleasing (*al-rāḍiya*).

However, the *sālik* does not see this Light consistently. He needs to know then that, at the moment he sees this color, his *nafs* is in one of these stations mentioned above.

The heart of the believer does not remain fixed; it moves and shifts from one state to another. Thus, his *nafs* is unstable. Imam Muslim reports in his *Ṣaḥīḥ* that the Prophet ﷺ said: "Hasten to perform good deeds, for there will come periods of trials and temptations like portions of a dark night. A man will be a believer in the morning and a disbeliever by the evening, or a believer in the evening and a disbeliever by the morning. He will sell his religion for the fleeting gains of this lower world."

This is why the disciple should not claim to have reached the accomplished *nafs* just because he has a vision of the purple Light. It is only at the moment of the vision that the disciple is in that station. The disciple should also remember that everything he attains is merely a grace from his Lord. Al-Tirmidhī reports in his *Sunan* from Anas Ibn Mālik that the Prophet would frequently say: "O You who turn the hearts, make my heart steadfast upon Your religion." Anas also said, "I asked: O Messenger of Allah! We have believed in you and in what you have brought. Do you fear for us?" The Prophet replied: "Yes, for indeed the hearts are between the two fingers of Allah; He turns them as He wills."

Thus, during his journey, the disciple will come to know the Names and Attributes of *jamāl* (beauty) as well as the Names and Attributes of *jalāl* (majesty), until his heart becomes fixed on the singular Name of Allah. This is where the point of realization lies.

*

Primary Colors and Their Shadows

Then the disciple recounts seeing in his vision a yellow color that tends toward white, as well as the following colors: purple, white, and yellow.

It is said that there are four primary colors. In reality, there are only three primary colors and four shadows of these colors, which gives us seven colors. Whoever grasps these colors grasps the secret of Allah ﷻ.

At this stage, the disciple should bring forth the name *al-Bāṭin* (The Concealed) to the name *al-Ẓāhir* (The Manifest Name), so that his heart becomes like a white snowball, as described in the hadith of the Prophet ﷺ.

The disciple can attain this through the name *al-Walī*, which corresponds to purple. This name flows through all the Names of Allah ﷻ. Allah ﷻ says in *Sūra* al-Baqara, verse 257: **"Allah is The Walī."**

Then the disciple sees a Light in the form of a semicircle resembling a wave moving in an ocean.

Whoever sees this should focus on the center of the vision to discern the blessed star of al-Muṣṭafā ﷺ.

*

The Body Is Directed by the Heart

One must understand that the diseases of the heart are more difficult and dangerous than the diseases of the body. The body is merely a vessel; it is secondary. The heart directs; the body moves only by the command of the heart. Know that the heart becomes corrupted when it is constantly directed toward worldly desires, such as the desire for food and drink, carnal desires, and the unlimited accumulation of worldly wealth.

This corrupted heart sends out a call to the other limbs of the body, turning them into something like Ya'jūj and

Ma'jūj (Gog and Magog). These people will emerge at the end of times to devour everything in their path. Therefore, it is imperative for a person to focus more on the heart than on the body. The primary goal for the heart is to attain vision and annihilation in Allah ﷻ. It is only under this influence that the body will follow the heart in the right direction.

*

What Does the Heart That Conceals All Secrets Represents, the One That Is in True *Tawḥīd*?

The word "heart" in Arabic is pronounced *qalb*. This word is written in Arabic as قلـب. The letter at the center of this word is the *lām* (ل). If we remove the *bā'* (ب), it gives us *qul* (قـل).

Allah ﷻ said to His chosen one ﷺ: "**Qul huwa Allāhu aḥad.**" This refers to *Sūra* al-Ikhlāṣ, where Allah ﷻ manifests His absolute oneness, the supreme manifestation of the Spirit in which all plurality dissolves.

This message is directed exclusively to Sayyidunā al-Muṣṭafā ﷺ as he represents his community. He ﷺ received the totality of the understanding of Allah's oneness. Allah ﷻ addresses him exclusively saying: "**Qul huwa Allāhu aḥad**" ("Say: 'He is Allah, One'"), because the speech spoken by the Prophet ﷺ is a supreme and transcendent one. It is the only speech that will truly bear witness to Allah's oneness, and that is why no other speech can surpass it. This is also why we say that the Prophet ﷺ is the interpreter of eternity.

*

Who Can Truly Understand *Tawḥīd*: The Unique Position of *Ahl al-Bayt*

The disciple will never fully comprehend this truth, yet he must surrender to it. Since the Prophet ﷺ embodied this truth, his words are a *sunna* (an example to follow). This transcendence in the blessed speech of al-Muṣṭafā ﷺ cannot be interpreted by the intellect of the disciple but by that of the Prophet ﷺ. His speech was transmitted as if it were the speech of the Qur'ān, for he is a walking Qur'ān, as our mother 'Ā'isha ﷺ described him.

As the ḥadīth emphasizes, his noble words contain four dimensions: an apparent dimension (*ẓāhir*), a hidden dimension (*bāṭin*), a dimension that extends to the limit of understanding (*ḥadd*), and an ascending dimension (*maṭlaʿ*). Just as there were four schools of jurisprudence, each one focused on interpreting the words of the Prophet ﷺ from one dimension. However, the elite of the family of the Prophet ﷺ inherited all the dimensions. We could also say that they inherited all the rings of the sciences of the Prophet ﷺ. They received it as a gift from the Prophet ﷺ and from his Lord ﷻ. They then shared this knowledge with those who followed them.

Imām al-Bukhārī ﷺ reports in his *Ṣaḥīḥ* that Abū Hurayra ﷺ said: "I received from the Messenger of Allah ﷺ two vessels of knowledge. I have transmitted one, and if I were to transmit the other, my throat would be cut." He thus received both exoteric and esoteric knowledge. Returning to the inheritance of the Prophet ﷺ: the knowledge of *Ahl al-Bayt*. this knowledge was confined within rings. The number of rings corresponds to the number of heavens, plus the Throne (*'arsh*) and the Pedestal (*Kursī*), totaling nine rings.

These nine rings of Light are the seat of esoteric knowledge. They are esoteric to us because the heavens, the Throne, and the Pedestal, from which they originate, are invisible to us and not located on earth. This can be illustrated with an example: suppose the disciple reaches the second heaven. At this station, the hidden sciences of the first heaven will be revealed to him. He then has to discover the esoteric sciences of the second heaven to move on to the third heaven.

The disciple must keep in mind that wherever he is, without the *idhn* (permission) of the Prophet ﷺ and without his intercession, he will never be able to encompass the full circumference of the ring. That is, he will not be able to comprehend the entirety of the knowledge contained within the ring of each heaven. He will only understand the portion that the *walī* has bequeathed to him, according to his position and his visibility within each ring. For example, some disciples may see 180 degrees of the circle, while others may see only 45.

Each person has their own vessel. However, the Prophet 卿, can intervene for a disciple and grant him the capacity to contain all 360 degrees of that circle. It is he 卿 who places the disciple at the center of the circle to make him understand all the degrees of a particular ring and to draw knowledge from it.

As for the disciple, he arrives on the path of Allah 卿 only seeing the perishable (*fānī*), for he himself is perishable. But the *walī*, who is the inheritor of the Prophet 卿, and the Prophet 卿 see everything. They have an open door to both the dimension of the perishable (*al-fanāʾ*) and the dimension of the enduring or imperishable (*al-baqāʾ*).

*

Indeed, He Who only Thinks of the Perishable Is Perishable

On the other hand, those who reject the words of the *walī* of Allah 卿 are those who believe only in the perishable. Their intellect is confined to the physical world, and they cannot conceive of an existing world beyond this physical realm.

To truly understand what is enduring, it is essential for the disciple to free himself from this mode of thinking limited to the physical. Indeed, he who only thinks of the perishable is perishable. He who persists in this way of thinking will come to believe that nature is God.

This is what is happening today in the West and even among some within the contemporary Muslim community. Many leave Islam because of this calamity. They begin to dig into the perishable until they conclude that the perishable is God!

These people are the true hypocrites, and Allah ﷻ has placed a wall between them and the true believers because they did not want to turn to the Prophet ﷺ, and therefore to his inheritor, Sayyidunā Alī ؏ to know the truth concealed behind this perishable world. Allah ﷻ says in *Sūra al-Ḥadīd*, verse 13: **"On the Day when the hypocrite men and women will say to those who believed, 'Wait for us that we may acquire some of your light.' It will be said, 'Go back behind you and seek light.' Then a wall will be placed between them with a door, its interior containing mercy, but on the outside, it will be facing punishment."**

*

Why Must One Who Seeks the Truth Go Through Sayyidunā 'Alī?

Sayyidunā 'Alī ؏ represents the door to al-Muṣṭafā ﷺ and he is the true manifestation of the letter *lām*.

Jābir ibn 'Abd Allāh ؓ reported that the Prophet ﷺ said: "I am the City of Knowledge, and 'Alī is its gate; whoever desires to enter the city must come through the gate." Commenting on this hadith, al-Ḥākim ؓ, in his

Mustadrak, said: "It is a *ṣaḥīḥ* (authentic) hadith according to its chain of transmission."

He is thus the only one who can truly project himself simultaneously into the perishable and enduring worlds. He is the isthmus (*barzakh*) between *baqā'* and *fanā'*.

This is why the Prophet ﷺ insists on loving Sayyidunā ʿAlī ﷺ. On the authority of ʿImrān ibn Ḥuṣayn ﷺ, the Messenger of Allah ﷺ said to Sayyidunā ʿAlī ﷺ: "Only a believer loves you, and only a hypocrite hates you." (reported by al-Ṭabarānī ﷺ in *al-Awsaṭ*) Sayyidunā ʿAlī ibn Abī Ṭālib ﷺ also said: "I swear by the One who split the grain and created life! This is indeed a covenant from the illiterate Messenger ﷺ: None but a believer loves me, and none but a hypocrite hates me." (reported by Muslim ﷺ in his *Ṣaḥīḥ*). Thus, the very source of hypocrisy is hatred for Sayyidunā ʿAlī ﷺ. It is through love for him that the disciple will reach the first heaven at the beginning of his journey. The heaven will then split open to grant the disciple access to the vision of the scarlet rose (*dihān*, meaning oil in Arabic) of Sayyida Fāṭima ﷺ.

Allah says in *Sūra* al-Raḥmān, verse 37: **"Then when the heaven is split asunder and becomes a rose, red like oil."**

*

What Does Sayyida Fāṭima Represent?

Sayyida Fāṭima ﷺ represents *al-dihān* (the oil) that emerges from this *warda* (the scarlet rose). It is she who illuminates without fire *al-shajara al-mubāraka* (the Blessed Tree), al-zaytūna (the Olive Tree), which is neither of the east nor of the west, transcending the laws of causality.

In his book *al-Iṣbāḥ*, Ibn Ḥajar al-ʿAsqalānī relates that Sayyida Fāṭima ﷺ was known as both the mother and the daughter of the Prophet ﷺ. Fāṭima ﷺ was nicknamed "the mother of her father" and was also known as *al-Zahrā'* (the Rose). It is as if Allah ﷻ is telling us that Sayyida Fāṭima ﷺ transcends all causality.

Thus, we can say that Sayyida Fāṭima ﷺ is the daughter of the Prophet ﷺ and we can also say that she is his mother! In reality, she is everything.

By deduction, the father of the Prophet ﷺ, is Sayyidunā ʿAlī ﷺ since he is her husband. In his book *Abundances*, al-Manāwī reports that the Prophet ﷺ, said: "ʿAlī is from me, and I am from ʿAlī, and only I or ʿAlī will guide me." This clearly shows that the relationship between the Prophet ﷺ, Sayyida Fāṭima ﷺ, and Sayyidunā ʿAlī ﷺ transcends all causality. It is beyond the grasp of confined intellect.

When the disciple listens to this discourse, his intellect begins to collapse, as it cannot grasp the nature of this relationship, which is perfectly defined by the verse of Light: **"A blessed olive tree, neither eastern nor western, whose oil would almost glow, even if untouched by fire."**

An oil that ignites without fire—this is the detail that our intellectual capacities cannot grasp. And this, in fact, represents the chain of transmission of the People of the Family of the Prophet ﷺ. Whoever is not connected to this chain of transmission (*sanad*) has no chain of transmission, for he is bound by causality and thus perishable. Therefore, in truth, his chain of transmission is nonexistent.

*

Lām

The letter *lām* is unique and different from all other letters of the Arabic language. Due to its power, it acquires supremacy over the other letters.

This is explained by its elevated chain of transmission. The *lām* consists of two consonants: the *lā* and the *mīm*. According to the chain (*sanad*) of the traditional Arabic alphabet, the *lā* corresponds to the number 30, and the *mīm* corresponds to the number 40. Among the people of Allah ﷻ, the *lā* refers to the Spirit, because Allah ﷻ begins with this letter in the testimony of His oneness: the total negation of all things, all creation, all plurality. *Lā*, then *illāha illā Allāh*.

In sum, the *lām* represents 30, and the *mīm* 40, which equates to the 70 branches (of the paths) of faith.

What does our beloved Prophet ﷺ say about these seventy branches? He ﷺ explains that the first branch is to remove obstacles from one's path, and the last is the knowledge of *lā illāha illā Allāh*. Only after this comes the perfect knowledge of the Spirit.

The *sālik* can only attain this after purifying his heart, at which point he becomes a divine first breath, and it is at this moment that he returns to his original station of spirit (*rūḥ*).

Thus, the one who becomes *rūḥ* returns to the command of Lordship (*rubūbiyya*).

The one who becomes the breath (*nafas*) of the Most-Merciful has also purified himself and returned to the command of the Most-Merciful (*al-Raḥmān*) but has not yet accessed the Spirit.

The Prophet ﷺ returned to his Lord. Indeed, *al-Raḥmān*, the Most-Merciful, is a name but also an attribute of Allah, which means that it leads us more toward the Attribute than the Essence. The Spirit, on the other hand, is of a lordly nature, and it annihilates us directly in the Essence of the Real.

*

The Core of Religion: *Lām* and *Bāʾ* (*lubb*)

We return to the heart to try to understand its secrets, particularly that of the *bāʾ* in the Arabic word *qalb* (قلب).

The Prophet ﷺ teaches us how to journey toward the "*bā*." This letter indeed represents his very being ﷺ. In *Ṭabaqāt al-Fuqahāʾ*, Abū Masʿūd al-Anṣārī ؓ reports that the Messenger of Allah ﷺ said: "Whoever prays a prayer without invoking blessings upon me and my family, it will not be accepted from him." That is to say, without the *lām*—the elite of the progeny of the Prophet—we can never know the "*bā*," the Prophet ﷺ.

On this subject, Imam al-Shāfiʿī ؆ explains: "Whoever does not invoke blessings upon the family of the Prophet ﷺ, his *ṣalāt* is not accepted!" This demonstrates that the one who removes the *lām* can never reach the *bāʾ*.

If we remove the *qāf* from the word *qalb* to understand the relationship between the *lām* and the *bāʾ*, we can read *lubb*. *Lubb* (لب) in Arabic means "core." The *ʿitra* of al-Muṣṭafā ﷺ is what connects the *lām* (inherited from the Prophet ﷺ) to the *bāʾ* (the Prophet ﷺ). These two letters are undoubtedly the inseparable core in this purification of the heart. Moreover, whoever has not connected himself to the *ʿitra* can never claim to have reached the truth of the Prophet ﷺ nor his *nūr*, and consequently, not the Spirit of the Real.

*

Who Is Connected to the *ʿItra* of the Prophet?

The Prophet ﷺ said: "*Ṣalāt* is light," and he also said: "*Ṣalāt* is the pillar of the religion," which means it is the core of the entire religion.

By deduction, the People of the Family of the Prophet ﷺ are the core of the religion since without invoking blessings upon them, our prayer would not be valid, as Imam al-Shāfiʿī ؆ clarifies.

If the servant does not accept them, he is not within the core of worship, and he will not be able to annihilate himself in the Spirit. Al-Muṣṭafā ﷺ bequeathed the path of Allah to them. That is, the People of the Family of the Prophet ﷺ.

According to Sayyidunā ʿAlī ibn Abī Ṭālib ؏: "I said: O Messenger of Allah, what were you created from? The Messenger of Allah ﷺ replied: 'When it was revealed to me by my Lord what was revealed to me, I said: O Lord, from what did You create me?' He said: 'By My Glory and Majesty, without you, I would not have created the earth or the heavens.' I said: 'Lord, from what did You create me?' He replied: 'O Muḥammad! I gazed upon the purity of the whiteness of My Light, which I had created with My Power, originated with My Wisdom, and added it in honor to My Greatness. I extracted a part of it and divided it into three sections. I created you and your family from the first section. Your wives and companions were created from the second section. And I created those who loved you from the third section. On the Day of Resurrection, I will return their Light into My Light and bring you, your family, your wives, your companions, and those who love you into Paradise with My Mercy. So, tell them about Me.'"

Al-Muṣṭafā ﷺ also said to Sayyidunā ʿAlī ؏: "My Light is from your Light, and your Light is from my Light."

*

The *Lām*, a Rope That Extends from Heaven to Earth

The *lām*, which connects the Prophet ﷺ to his descendants, as we have seen before, is also described in the hadith of *al-thaqalayn* (the hadith about following the *'itra* and the Book) as the rope of Light that stretches from the heavens to the earth. If the word of Allah is written on earth, it is not written in the heavens. Indeed, in the heavens, we move beyond the framework of written letters or the physical nature of letters to discover the spirit of the word.

The wayfarer (*sālik*) must therefore cling to this rope, which is the *lām*, in order to ascend in the Spirit of the Qur'ān. He must thus leave behind earthly gravity. To achieve this, he will need the Light, which manifests through the *'itra*, who, as we have demonstrated, are the core of the religion and the very Spirit of the blessed Qur'ān.

*

Qubb

If we then remove the *lām* from the word *qalb*, we get the word *qubb* (قُـبّ). In the Arabic language, this word means "a container," or more precisely "a dome." And since the dome is directed towards the sky, we can say that the *qubb* is a celestial container. This container is, moreover, the very heart of the believer. By its celestial nature, it will be the chair of the *lām*, the rope that extends from the heavens to the earth. Therefore, for the disciple to claim that he carries a living heart, his container must be celestial. It must not, consequently, be darkened and rusted by earthly vices.

Imām al-Tirmidhī ﷛ reports in his *Sunan*, on the authority of Sayyidunā 'Abd Allāh ibn 'Umar ﷛ that the Messenger of Allah ﷺ said: "Your hearts become rusted like iron touched by water." The companions asked him how to clean them. He ﷺ replied: "By frequent remembrance of death and recitation of the Qur'ān."

Rusted hearts cannot be celestial; they are drawn to the earth, they are rusted and damaged. Now, you need to know, o disciple, that the celestial *qubb*, which will receive the *lām*, will grant its bearer the 70 secrets and thus the 7 readings. This disciple will have a *wijha* (a direction) towards what is perishable, towards servitude (*'ubūdiyya*), and a *wijha* towards what is existent/real, towards Lordship (*rubūbiyya*).

Simultaneously, he will also have a *wijha* towards the Qur'ān and a *wijha* towards *ahl al-bayt*, the People of the Family of the Prophet ﷺ. Thus, claiming to be a believer is no longer enough, nor is merely saying that we love the People of the Family of the Prophet ﷺ for indeed every word conceals a truth.

Whoever omits to connect to the *wasīṭa* (intermediary), that is to the *lām*, and yet utters these words, is either a liar or ignorant of their true weight.

Indeed, to access the love of the People of the Family of the Prophet ﷺ, a Muslim must find the *lām* of his time, the one who connects the heavens to the earth. The Muslim who denies it also denies by necessity the Book, for it is the very Spirit of the Book. This Muslim cannot claim to love the People of the Family of the Prophet ﷺ.

On the contrary, his rejection of the *lām* will lead him to become the enemy of the *walī*. And let the one who becomes the enemy of the *walī* know that Allah takes him as an enemy. War is thus declared against him by the Lord, as the sacred hadith emphasizes. In *Ṣaḥīḥ al-Bukhārī*, Sayyidunā Abū Hurayra ﷺ reports that in the *ḥadīth qudsī*, Allah ﷻ says: "Whoever shows enmity to a *walī* of Mine, I declare war against him."

The one who denies the *lām* says unknowingly: "I do not need the *lām* in my *qalb*" or "I want to leave my heart empty." The empty heart becomes the enemy of Allah ﷻ. By removing the *lām* from the word *qalb*, only *qubb* remains, leaving behind a mere empty container.

*

The *Lām*: The Vital Connection Between *Lā* and *Mīm*

The Karkarī disciple has developed a passion for the *lām* only because this *lām* has been confined within the *mīm* of al-Muṣṭafā ﷺ. The *lām* could only attain this supremacy through the *mīm* of al-Muṣṭafā ﷺ. And it is only because of this letter that we have the possibility of seeing the *walī* in the perishable world. (Without the *mīm*, the *walī* would have remained in the *bāṭin* (the concealed) or in his transcendent reality (*ḥaqīqa*), which is total extinction in the Spirit of his Lord).

On the other hand, when we pronounce the "*lā*," we are in the total negation of all plurality, which elevates us to the *maqām* of the *rūḥ* (the Spirit). This total negation, which is the *rūḥ*, was enraptured by the *mīm* of al-Muṣṭafā ﷺ.

According to the chain of transmission, the *mīm* represents the number 40. It is the seat of the 40 *nufūs* (sg. *nafs*) gathered in the seven mother *nufūs*. The *mīm* is considered the representation of all the stations of the *nafs*.

The *lām* is a letter pronounced from the *bāṭin*, that is, from the depth or the heart, like all the letters of *lā ilāha illā Allāh*. All these letters come from the depths of the heart of the believer in Allah. Whoever does not carry the *lām* in his heart finds himself with an emptied heart; its depth is rusted, and it has no *wijha* towards the Spirit. When he dies, he will not be able to pronounce the *shahāda* or *lā ilāha illā Allāh*.

The servant will never enter Islam without pronouncing the continuation of the formula *Muḥammad rasūl Allāh*. The direction towards the Messenger ﷺ, that is, the *mīm*, is also obligatory.

The same sanctity must be given to both, that is, to the Spirit, the *lām*, and to the Messenger, the *mīm* ﷺ. Allah ﷻ has linked His Oneness with the Message. They are complementary and inseparable.

When the servant of Allah says with his heart *lā ilāha illā Allāh*, it is indeed not he who says it! It is the Messenger ﷺ within his *nafs*, who pronounces this formula.

Allah ﷻ says in *Sūra* al-Tawba: **"A Messenger has come to you from your own *nafs*."**

And let the disciple finally know that when We emerged from Our spiritual seclusion (*khulwa*), the first thing We said was: "I have returned to Allah and then Allah guided me to my Shaykh. O, it is me, my Shaykh! O, my Shaykh."

Session XII
December 18, 2020

*

The Disciple's Obligation to Fulfill the First Reading

The Friday sessions always focused on the first secret of the second reading. We remind that the Karkari disciple journeys through the reading of the Name Allah. To this day, the disciples have completed the first seven secrets of the first reading. Sīdī Shaykh started revealing the first secret of the second reading in June 2020. This secret is manifested through Sūra Ṭā Hā. The disciple will thus experience this secret through this Sūra. Meanwhile, Sīdī Shaykh held a session every Friday where he provided an exegesis of this Sūra, so that we could understand how to grasp the secret. We have reached verses 39 and 40: **"And I bestowed upon you love from Me that you would be brought up under My eye. Remember when your sister came along and proposed, 'Shall I direct you to one who will nurse him?'"**

In *Ṣaḥīḥ al-Bukhārī*, Sayyidunā Abū Hurayra ﷺ narrates that the Messenger of Allah ﷺ said: "Allah said: My servant continues to draw near to Me with voluntary acts until I love him."

This part of the hadith aligns with the *ḥadīth qudsī* in which Allah ﷻ says: "I was a hidden treasure, and I loved to be known (...)."

When we read these two hadiths, we understand how Sayyidunā Mūsā ﷺ was captivated by this love of Allah ﷻ. He obtained this love even when the Divine was a hidden treasure, that is, from pre-eternity. He was elected and loved by Allah ﷻ. His appearance in the physical world is the result of this flow from pre-eternity, which manifested in this form (*Ṣūra*). This flow represents the love we speak of, which appeared as a *Ṣūra* in the world of the perishable.

Know that Sayyidunā Mūsā ﷺ is *ḥabīb Allāh* (the beloved of Allah). He is thus the elect of Allah. He was loved by Allah ﷻ even before knowing that Allah ﷻ loved him. That is why, when he stood before the mighty presence (*ḥaḍra*) of the Most Holy (*al-Quddūs*), Allah ﷻ unlocked the gateways of *fatḥ* (spiritual opening) for him. It was then that he understood that Allah ﷻ had opened the doors of love for him, showing him that He loved him. And if Allah ﷻ loves you, He will also open your spiritual eye, the eye of *fatḥ*, as He did for Sayyidunā Mūsā ﷺ.

When you arrive at the Shaykh, you may think you know the causes that brought you to him, but in truth, this is false. Everything you did before arriving here was created by Allah ﷻ. It is He ﷻ who created you, who loved you in pre-eternity, and thus brought you to His Light. It is He ﷻ who made you journey toward Him! This did not come from your own will! It is not by your own volition but by Allah ﷻ, by His will and His unique power.

That is why the first thing we must do is say *al-ḥamdu lillāh* (praise be to Allah) that we are Muslims and part of the Muslim community.

Besides choosing you from among humanity to be part of this selection, He also chose you within this selection and selected you among those who love the Prophet ﷺ, and whom the Prophet ﷺ loves.

You are part of the best community that Allah has created. The people of Israel in the time of Sayyidunā Mūsā عليه السلام or the Christians and those who lived in the era of Sayyidunā ʿĪsā عليه السلام were also *muwaḥḥidūn* (monotheists). They knew that Allah ﷻ is One, but they did not have access to the secret of *tawḥīd al-jamʿ* (the secret of union). They did not have what the Muslims received by the grace of the Lord. Indeed, the Muslim has the privilege of being among the community of the one who united and gathered the Prophets in his heart, that is, Sayyidunā Muḥammad ﷺ. For example, the Prophet ʿĪsā عليه السلام is but one facet of al-Muṣṭafā ﷺ and thus his people only had the knowledge emanating from that facet.

Allah ﷻ gave this Muslim community the completeness of knowledge, and this is a sign of limitless love and another favor that the pre-Islamic monotheistic peoples did not receive. To summarize, Allah ﷻ has blessed this community with the secret of total union, as well as access to all the sciences of differentiation (*farq*) in their most complete form—that is, access to the city of knowledge, which is the city of al-Muṣṭafā ﷺ. Thus, the Muslim has access to the *ḥaqīqa*, the ultimate truth, and to the most complete *sharīʿa*.

That is why the Muslim has the obligation to access at least the first secret of *jamʿ*, or at least the first reading. Every Muslim must possess this first secret.

Among the people of realization (*taḥqīq*), the journey must proceed in this way. Whoever has not acquired the first reading has not fulfilled an obligation.

*

The Heart That Contained Him

Then Allah ﷻ says: **"And that you would be brought up under My eye."** Imam al-Ghazālī ﷺ reports in his book *Iḥyāʾ ʿulūm al-dīn* that the Messenger of Allah ﷺ said in the *ḥadīth qudsī*: "Neither My earth nor My heavens can contain Me... Only the gentle heart of My believing servant has contained Me."

If the disciple were to focus and meditate on this hadith, he could extract pearls from it.

Know that everything you see—all these heavens, all these earths—could not contain Allah ﷻ. Only the heart of the believing servant (*muʾmin*) has contained Him.

This heart, then, is the throne of Allah ﷻ. That is why one should not think with the intellect—that is, through the *nafs*—but rather through the heart. This heart, which bears the throne of Allah ﷻ sees nothing but the proximity of Allah ﷻ. It inclines solely in search of His nearness ﷻ and yearns for that proximity and nothing else.

Unfortunately, the heart of the one who desires paradise has not contained Allah ﷻ; it has become the throne of paradise, a creation of Allah. And the heart of the one who fears the fire has become the throne of fear, doing everything out of fear to avoid the fire. This heart too has become the throne of a creation, unlike the heart of the *mu'min*, which is the throne of the Creator.

We can understand the nature of our heart by aligning it with this revealing logic. It is then that the servant can understand which category his heart belongs to.

Let us return to the story of Sayyidunā Mūsā عليه السلام. His mother abandoned him in a small chest on the Nile. This chest floated up the river until it reached the shore near Pharaoh's palace. There, the palace servants found it and decided to bring it back to be adopted. At that precise moment, the sister of Sayyidunā Mūsā عليه السلام approached them to direct them to someone who could care for him. And thus, he returned to his mother through pure mercy.

It is also known that the vizier of Sayyidunā Mūsā عليه السلام, the one who always supported him in his adulthood, was his elder brother, Sayyidunā Hārūn عليه السلام. However, the Qur'ānic text shows us that when Sayyidunā Mūsā عليه السلام was still an infant, it was his sister who played this role of support. She was the vizier of Sayyidunā Mūsā ﷺ when he was weak. Sayyidunā Hārūn ﷺ would take on this role later. All of this flows in a single direction: the complete devotion of Sayyidunā Mūsā's family to the master of the divine assembly (*ḥaḍra*) of their time, who was none other than Sayyidunā Mūsā ﷺ. This perfectly explains how Sayyidunā Mūsā ﷺ was brought up under the watchful eye of Allah ﷻ.

Allah ﷻ further clarifies this detail in the reported events. Even Pharaoh, the sworn enemy of the *ḥaḍra*, became the servant of the Vicegerent (*khalīfa*) of his time without even realizing it. He welcomed him, fed him, and raised him, only for Mūsā ﷺ to later become the cause of his downfall.

Allah ﷻ then says: **"Then We returned you to your mother."** That is to say, We returned you to your first truth! The first truth of Sayyidunā Mūsā ﷺ appeared when he was in his blessed mother's womb.

Indeed, she received the revelation of Sayyidunā Mūsā's prophecy before his birth, knowing that her son would be a Prophet and Messenger. She was also instructed to place him on the Nile, allowing him to drift until he reached a place where he would be safe from Pharaoh's slaughter of the children of Israel. In contrast, Sayyidunā ʿĪsā ﷺ proclaimed his prophecy and message to the people of Israel while still an infant. That is why his mother Maryam ﷺ would turn to him for guidance. However, with Sayyidunā Mūsā ﷺ, it was his mother who bore the truth of the message and acted on his behalf.

To better understand this comparison between the two *ḥaḍra*, know that when Sayyidunā Mūsā ﷺ was born, he manifested the Name *al-Bāṭin* (the Concealed). As for his mother, she manifested the Name *al-Ẓāhir* (the Apparent). It was she who revealed his message.

On the other hand, it was Sayyidunā ʿĪsā ﷺ himself who revealed his message. He was the bearer of the name *al-Ẓāhir*, and his mother Maryam ﷺ manifested the Name *al-Bāṭin* from the beginning of his story. This is evident in the narrative of the two *ḥaḍra*.

*

The Notion of Centrality

Mūsā ﷺ was the center of the *ḥaḍra mūsāwiyya*, meaning the center of all manifestations of his time. And it was indeed he who, in truth, caused the revelation to appear to his mother, so that she could manifest the trace of the name *al-Ẓāhir* (the Apparent). That is why she decided to place him ﷺ in the river, entrusting him to the holy spiritual assembly (*ḥaḍra*). Then, Allah made what is *bāṭin* (hidden), that is Mūsā ﷺ return to his mother, so that the message of Allah would be revealed.

In *Sūra* Ṭāhā, verse 40, Allah ﷻ says: **"Thus, We returned him to his mother so that she might find comfort."**

Know that the mother of Mūsā ﷺ was very sad when she parted from him. This reminds us of the story of

Prophet Ya'qūb ﷵ when he was separated from his son Sayyidunā Yūsuf ﷵ. Indeed, Prophet Yūsuf ﷵ represented the core reality (*ḥaqīqa*) of his father, just as Sayyidunā Mūsā ﷵ represented the core reality of his mother.

Her heart became empty because she was no longer in the companionship of the *wasīṭa* (intermediary). She was no longer with the *lām* of her time. And it was only when the *lām* returned to her that she breathed and found rest.

Know that the letter *lām* in the word *qalb* (قلب) (heart) is located in the middle. The placement of this letter in the middle gives us two facets of the Truth. The letter *lām* separates the letters *qāf* and *bā'*. If we connect the *qāf* with the *lām*, we obtain *qul*, which means "Say." This represents the Apparent, that is, the *sharī'a*. However, if we connect the *lām* with the *bā'*, we obtain *lubb*, which means "core" and represents the *ḥaqīqa*. In truth, the one who has no *lām* in his heart retains only the word *qubb*. And *qubb* in Arabic means "empty vessel." A *qalb* without a *lām* is a *qubb*, and thus represents an empty vessel. Know also that any vessel not filled with the *nūr* of Allah ﷻ is directed towards perversity.

Let us return to this breakdown of the word *qalb*, which gives us three aspects:

– *Qul* represents the *sharī'a* (jurisprudence), the exoteric knowledge.

– *Lubb* represents the *ḥaqīqa*, "core truth" or esoteric knowledge.

– *Qubb* represents perversity.

Know that if the wayfarer denies the *wasīṭa*, the *lām* in his heart becomes empty because the *lām* is a cord that descends from the heavens to the earth. And know also that every person has the trace of the *lām* in his heart; even those who do not believe in Allah ﷻ for they cannot pronounce something that is not within their heart.

When we enter the spiritual path, we understand that we are merely returning backwards. It is as if we are ascending towards our truth. We only have the illusion of moving forward. Everything we experience is but a trace of the truth, a truth that was engraved in us in pre-eternity (*al-qidam*) by our Lord ﷻ. An example may clarify what we have just described: in reality, a person will learn many languages because, in *al-azal*, Allah ﷻ gave them the capacity to learn them. The causes that lead to the acquisition of this learning are ultimately predetermined by this divine pre-eternal capacity.

In practice, this person will only manifest what Allah ﷻ has placed in his heart.

However, the dilemma lies in the fact that as long as we have not exited the confinement of time and space, we cannot escape the prison of causality and return to the capacity and power of Allah ﷻ, who wrote everything before the cause even existed. In truth, causes (*asbāb*, sg. *sabab*) are nonexistent, or, more precisely, the cause exists only in our confined and delimited intellect. Why is this the case? This is because we are in continuous denial of the fact that the Capacity/Power of Allah ﷻ is the only truth.

To summarize, the *lām* always represents the *wasīṭa*, that is, the intermediary between the Lord and the servant. It serves as a doorway that opens onto two dimensions: one facing the transient, the realm of nonexistence, and the other facing the existent, the eternal realm—the City of Knowledge, which is the City of the Prophet ﷺ.

*

How Did Mūsā Reach Realization?

In *Sūra* Ṭāhā, verse 40, Allah ﷻ says: **"Then you killed a man, but We delivered you from the distress that overwhelmed you, and We tested you with various trials. You remained for years among the people of Madyan. Then you came, O Mūsā, according to Our decree."**

In reality, although the outward act seemed directed towards another, the self that Mūsā السلام truly killed was his own. If not for this act, he would have remained confined within Pharaoh's palace, trapped in a life of luxury that would have hindered his spiritual realization. His flight to the *falā'*, as mentioned in the Noble Qur'ān, marked a profound transformation. The *falā'* in Arabic signifies a vast, empty expanse. In the story of Mūsā السلام, it refers to the immense desert of Sinai, stretching between Egypt and Palestine. However, in this *ḥaḍra*, the *falā'* represents *al-iṭlāq*, the Absolute—like the hadith of the ring in an endless space: *ḥalāqa fī falā'*. It was within this boundless expanse that Sayyidunā Mūsā ﷺ encountered Sayyidunā Shuʿayb ﷺ who became his Shaykh, the heart guiding him on his journey to spiritual realization.

*

Why Did Allah Name Him Shuʿayb?

The name Shuʿayb comes from the root *shuʿba*, and the word *shuʿba* in Arabic means a branch. In his *Ṣaḥīḥ*, Imam al-Bukhārī ﷺ reports from Sayyidunā Abū Hurayra ﷺ that the Prophet ﷺ said: "Faith has more than sixty or seventy branches (*shaʿba*). The best of them is the declaration that there is no deity worthy of worship except Allah, and the least of them is removing harm from the path. Modesty is also a branch of faith."

Sayyidunā Shuʿayb ﷺ thus, in truth, represents the branches (*shuʿab*) of faith (*al-īmān*). He is therefore the Shaykh of Mūsā ﷺ, and he will help him understand the concealed sciences within the branches of faith.

The self that Mūsā ﷺ previously killed was thus the door through which he returned to Allah ﷺ. We cannot say that Mūsā ﷺ was not with his Lord before this event. However, it allowed him to accelerate his spiritual journey, despite the fact that, in the apparent (not in truth), it was a grave sin.

Ibn ʿAṭāʾ Allāh al-Iskandarī ﷺ said in his *Ḥikam*: "A sin that begets humility and need is better than obedience that begets pride and arrogance!"

Mūsā ﷵ killed, and that is why he repented. He entered the *ḥaḍra* of his Lord through the gateway of repentance. This is always the same story that repeats itself: the one who enters through the gateway of repentance and carries in his heart the burden of a life full of sins will succeed in the spiritual journey. Allah ﷻ shows us this sunna in the story of Mūsā ﷵ, who regretted killing. This is how Mūsā ﷵ was able to receive the esoteric sciences. And that is why most disciples who succeed in the spiritual journey are those who were in sin.

We do not say that Mūsā ﷵ committed a sin—far from it—for the Prophets are protected from such acts. However, Allah ﷻ showed us, the real sinners, this example so that we may learn from it.

However, the one who has always engaged in good deeds, in prayer, and stands in the front row in the mosque often considers himself close to Allah ﷻ and may not recognize the evil within him. How can he be brought closer to Allah ﷻ if he already believes he is near? Meanwhile, the one who approaches filled with sins sees himself as unworthy, distant, humiliated, and weak. He perceives no escape except through the Mercy of Allah ﷻ. Thus, he surrenders himself completely to Him ﷻ.

Outwardly, this person comes to the Shaykh seeking knowledge of Allah ﷻ, yet his heart tells him he is unworthy of such knowledge. Deep down, all he truly asks for is that Allah ﷻ grants him repentance, forgiveness, and contentment. This is the type of disciple who will succeed on the spiritual journey.

*

Do not Be Like the *A'rāb* (bedouins)

In the *ḥaḍra Muḥammadiyya*, the Companions of the Prophet ﷺ played the role of Sayyidunā Hārūn عليه السلام in the *ḥaḍra Mūsawiyya*, when it came to conveying the words and teachings of the Prophet ﷺ to the Bedouins (*a'rāb*). The Companions truly loved the Prophet ﷺ. They always adorned themselves with *adab* (proper manners) in his presence and towards the people of his family ﷺ. This sunna continued with a group from the *salaf* and some of those who came after them.

It is also known in the *sīra* (the life of the Prophet ﷺ) that the Bedouins often lacked proper manners with the Prophet ﷺ. This is why they sought their knowledge from his Companions, may Allah be pleased with them.

Those who truly love the Prophet ﷺ and the people of his family ﷺ seek knowledge directly from his Gate, represented by Sayyidunā 'Alī عليه السلام.

Al-Ḥākim, in his *Mustadrak*, relates this authentic hadith where Jābir ibn 'Abd Allāh ﷺ reports the Prophet ﷺ saying: "I am the city of knowledge, and 'Alī is its gate; whoever desires to reach the city must pass through the gate."

Those who harbor dislike for the people of the Prophet's family, *ahl al-bayt*, mostly follow the Companions today, but they fail to follow the elite of the Progeny of the Chosen One ﷺ. Those who refuse to take knowledge from the people of the family of the Prophet ﷺ and do not follow them are, in truth, hypocrites. Do these people not remind us of the *Wahhābīs* of our time?

*

Da'wa that Becomes an Obstacle to *Dhikr* Is Invalid

Let us return to *Sūra* Ṭāhā, where Allah ﷻ says in verses 42 to 44: **"Go, you and your brother, with My signs; and do not neglect to remember Me."**

Allah ﷻ tells Prophet Mūsā ﷵ and Prophet hārūn ﷵ to invoke Him constantly while going to do *da'wa* to Pharaoh. You need to know disciples that the one who does *da'wa*, yet it becomes an obstacle between him and the *dhikr* of Allah ﷻ, between him and the vision of Allah's light, and between him and the secrets of Allah ﷻ, must know that his *da'wa* is not valid. Allah ﷻ is essentially telling Mūsā ﷵ, "When you go to Pharaoh to do da'wa and bring him back to Me, remember that I am your intermediary (*wasīṭa*), and you go for My sake."

The disciple should strive to be in a state of witnessing the *nūr* when engaging in *da'wa*. In this state, he performs it for Allah ﷻ and under His benevolent gaze, for the *nūr* can only emanate from Him ﷻ, and it serves as a concrete sign of His blessed Presence. During *da'wa*, the disciple may also witness the Bright Star, the illuminating torch, which truly represents the Prophet ﷺ. This disciple can consider himself as being under the compassionate gaze of al-Muṣṭafā ﷺ. If this direct witnessing is not possible, he should always hold the intention in his heart to perform this *daʿwa* for the *wasīṭa*, as it will invariably guide him back to the luminous exemplifications.

*

Hārūn: The Interpreter of Truth

Sayyidunā Mūsā ﷺ had annihilated himself in his Lord. The mission of Sayyidunā Hārūn ﷺ was to convey through speech to Pharaoh that his brother had annihilated himself in his Lord. Mūsā ﷺ was so immersed in the truth and had mastered such elevated realities that he required someone to communicate these profound concepts to Pharaoh and the people of Israel, who were themselves quite limited in understanding. It was in this precise context that Hārūn ﷺ assumed the role of interpreter of the divine assembly (*ḥaḍra*).

*

Gentleness in *Daʿwa* in the Face of Tyranny

Allah ﷻ says in verses 44 and 45 of the same *Sūra*: "Go to Pharaoh, for he has indeed transgressed (*ṭaghā*). But speak to him gently; perhaps he may take heed or come to fear [Me]."

Pharaoh had indeed become a despot (*ṭaghā*), and Allah ﷻ further clarifies in *Sūra* al-Baqara, verse 257:

"**Allah is the *Walī* of those who have faith; He brings them out of the darknesses into the light. As for those who disbelieve, their *walīs* are the despots (*ṭāghūt*), who lead them out of the light into the darknesses.**"

Pharaoh had become a soldier of Iblīs, fully embodying this verse: "**As for those who disbelieve, their *walīs* are the despots (*ṭāghūt*), who lead them out of the light into the darknesses.**"

Yet despite all this tyranny, Allah ﷻ commands Mūsā ﷻ to approach this soldier of Iblīs with the utmost gentleness.

This message is for all of us! Whoever is present with Allah ﷻ can never allow himself to speak harshly to others, even if faced with violent opposition. Reflect on the greatness of Sayyidunā Mūsā ﷺ. He was not calling just anyone to the Light, but the greatest tyrant of his time. And yet, Sayyidunā Mūsā ﷺ addressed him with gentleness. This divine command is a reminder for all of us in how we invite others to the Light.

We must always carry out *daʿwa* in the manner of Mūsā ﷺ, never with harshness. Only then can we attract hearts toward the *walī*.

Session XIII
23 December 2020

*

Dreaming of a Swamp, a Stream, or Similar

A female disciple shared a vision (mushāhada) she had during the morning wird. In her vision, she saw herself running after a person who entered a dark forest. This person crossed a swamp. Trying to follow, the disciple attempted to cross as well, but monstrous creatures emerged from the swamp.

The vision of a swamp, the sea, or anything similar represents the *dunyā*. When a disciple swims and crosses a body of water, it signifies that he has passed through this *dunyā* and is saved. As for the one who sees himself struggling to swim and has difficulty crossing, it indicates that he will likely have great difficulty surpassing this *dunyā*. Finally, the one who drowns in the dream will face significant challenges in passing the trials of this *dunyā*.

*

Following the Light by Clinging to Its Source

This disciple also saw herself running after someone. She followed this person, who led her to the aforementioned place. This means she is following someone who is guiding her toward error. This reminds us of the steps of Shayṭān (Satan). Indeed, to lure someone, Shayṭān leads him down various paths that Allah ﷻ dislikes, in order to cause him to fall. The goal is to vary the paths of misguidance until they lead the person to acts displeasing to Allah ﷻ. Whoever refuses to be with such a person and desires to be saved must have the Light. He must follow this Light and the one who gave it to him.

This Light is the gateway to *taqwā* (God-consciousness) and *ikhlāṣ* (sincerity) toward Allah ﷻ. It is reported in *Ṭabaqāt al-Shāfiʿiyya* by Imam Tāj al-Dīn al-Subkī that al-Junayd ﷺ said, "Sincerity is a secret between Allah and the servant. No angel has access to it to write it down, no demon knows it to spoil it, and no desire knows it to corrupt it."

There is also a *ḥadīth qudsī* that al-Qushayrī ﷺ reported with his chain of transmission reaching the Lord of Glory ﷻ: "Sincerity is one of My secrets. I place it in the heart of those I love among My servants." The Light is also a secret between the Lord and His servants. Thus, sincerity (*ikhlāṣ*) toward Allah ﷻ is a Light.

Shayṭān cannot perceive nor damage this Light. Even the angels cannot have access to it to record it. As long as the disciple turns toward the one who gave him the Light—that is, the *walī*, who is his *qibla*—no one can make him stumble onto the wrong paths of Shayṭān. But if he disperses his attention and associates with multiple shaykhs, Shayṭān will send him from one shaykh to another until he falls into acts detested by Allah ﷻ.

Know that the one who leads the disciple into the city of al-Muṣṭafā ﷺ, is not just anyone. Indeed, al-Ḥākim ؓ reports in his *Mustadrak* that Sayyidunā Jābir ibn ʿAbd Allāh ؓ related that the Prophet ﷺ said: "I am the city of knowledge, and ʿAlī is its gate. Whoever desires to enter the city must go through the gate."

Therefore, there is only one gate to reach the city of Sayyidunā al-Muṣṭafā ﷺ and that is Sayyidunā ʿAlī ؑ. Whoever claims there are multiple gates is speaking without knowledge and contradicts the hadith of the Prophet ﷺ.

Only the renewer (*mujaddid*), who is sent every hundred years as specified in the hadith, can guide the wayfarer to the city of knowledge. But if the wayfarer seeks to enter this city through a gate other than that of Sayyidunā ʿAlī ؑ, he will find nothing but monsters.

The one who will bring the disciple to this city is the one who achieved realization in the knowledge of Allah ﷻ. The one who claims to be knowledgeable and a gateway for others, yet stumbles and commits errors, will bear the burden of his own sins and those of others who followed him down that path, whereas the ordinary Muslim who commits an error will only bear his own.

This is why the Prophet ﷺ emphasized the importance of carefully choosing one's imam, for they intercede on behalf of those who follow them. It is therefore our duty not to follow just any imam, for if he lacks Light on the Day of Judgment, he may lead those who followed him into ruin.

Al-Dāraquṭnī and al-Bayhaqī ﷺ report that the Prophet ﷺ said: "Your imams are your intercessors before Allah. If you want to purify your prayers, then appoint the best among you."

*

Meditation Must Be Accompanied by *Dhikr*

Another disciple, originally from Algeria, reported seeing a dream in which an insect emerged from between her eyes. The spot where the insect emerged began to burn.

Allah ﷻ describes in the Qur'an the *nāṣiya* (forelock) as the location of lying and sin. Anatomically, the *nāṣiya* corresponds to the frontal lobe, the part of the brain associated with intellect. The disciple should know that everything that emerges from the intellect is inherently false and erroneous.

Reflecting and meditating without *dhikr* leads to exceeding the limits set by Allah ﷻ as the people of Allah have emphasized. Reflection must always be accompanied by *dhikr*, for one who engages in reflection without *dhikr* engages the part of the intellect that Allah ﷻ has described as deceitful and always in error.

Today, Muslims are so influenced by Westerners that they have abandoned reflection with *dhikr* and instead cling to the lies that stem from reflection without *dhikr*, following the Western way. They are not far from Buddhists, Hindus, and yoga practitioners. These, along with all who approve of them, are in sin.

Allah ﷻ describes in the Qur'ān how one should reflect. In *Sūra* Āl ʿImrān, verses 190 and 191, Allah ﷻ says: **"Indeed, in the creation of the heavens and the earth and the alternation of the night and the day are signs for those of understanding, who remember Allah while standing, sitting, and lying on their sides, and reflect on the creation of the heavens and the earth, saying, 'Our Lord, You did not create this aimlessly; exalted are You; protect us from the punishment of the Fire.'"**

Thus, the disciple must ensure that he remembers Allah abundantly without interruption, regardless of his location or position.

We have a perfect example of this in the companion of the Prophet ﷺ, Sayyidunā Abū Bakr al-Ṣiddīq ﵁. He engaged in so much *dhikr* that when he went to the restroom, he would put pebbles in his mouth to prevent his tongue from invoking Allah ﷻ. He did this because he held great reverence (*taʿẓīm*) for Allah ﷻ and His remembrance.

Whoever reaches a state of constant *dhikr* will engage in it even while sleeping and dreaming. Upon waking, the first thing he will do is *dhikr*. His tongue will never cease from *dhikr*. This is the first stage that the *sālik* must pass through when he enters the path.

Disciples who engaged in abundant *dhikr* before reaching the *walī* were prepared by Allah ﷻ to receive the Light. Their journey will be easier. The first *dhikr* a disciple should practice is *istighfār*. This is how he will revive his heart.

After this initial stage, he should start engaging in reflection (*tafakkur*). Allah ﷻ informs us how this should be performed. One should begin by reflecting on how Allah ﷻ created the heavens and the earth, not on what is contained within them.

Moreover, *tafakkur* should focus first on the heavens, not the earth. One should ask how Allah ﷻ created the first heaven, then the second heaven, and so on until reaching the creation of the seventh heaven. Only after this should the disciple begin to meditate on the earth.

Initially, one should not meditate on the earth and its constituents, such as trees, animals, or stones, but solely on how they were created by Allah ﷻ.

The *sālik* must reflect comprehensively on the creation of the heavens and the earth. He should ask questions about the age of the earth and how it was created from Light. In this way, he will come to understand the history of the earth without resorting to experimental science, which stems from the *nāṣiya* and is therefore erroneous. However, this can only be achieved while in a state of continuous *dhikr*.

Here are some other questions the disciple may also ask during his *dhikr*: Which heaven was created before the others? Was the earth created before the heavens?

Unfortunately, when the *sālik* enters the path, he does not engage in enough *dhikr*. This is why he is unable to answer these questions.

*

How Does Allah Purify Our *Nafs* from Its Vices?

Let us return to the disciple's dream. The insect that came out from between the disciple's eyes is comparable to a bacteria or a virus. The disciple should know that the greatest bacteria that can afflict a person is arrogance, as well as thinking oneself better than others. Burning this insect is good news for this disciple.

Allah ﷻ purifies the *nafs* through *sujūd*, the act of prostrating in His presence. This is why Muslims prostrate during prayer. By placing the forehead in contact with the ground, the lowest of places, the disciple humbles himself before his Lord instead of being arrogant. This is also why, during prayer, a Muslim must focus on the point of *sujūd*, as looking elsewhere disrupts the prayer.

To burn the spiritual bacteria, insects, vices, and *shayāṭīn*, one must remain in continuous *dhikr*. Thus, Allah ﷻ will burn the viruses and insects of the *nāṣiya* and bestow His knowledge. From that point on, everything the disciple says will come from the heart of the Prophet ﷺ and he will never go astray again.

*

Enduring Trials on the Path of Allah

This same disciple then saw herself buying two units of dark chocolate, and on his way, one unit fell to the ground. It got slightly damaged, but he picked it up and continued walking. Of these two units of chocolate, one was for him, and the other was for his family. When he arrived home, he felt at peace.

Seeing oneself taking something sweet in a dream signifies receiving *rizq* (provision). *Rizq* is not necessarily something material. On the contrary, the greatest *rizq* is the knowledge of Allah ﷻ (*al-maʿrifa*). We can always associate the vision of sweet foods with *maʿrifa*, as sweets (*ḥalwā*) were among the things the Prophet ﷺ loved to eat. Moreover, the darker the chocolate, the purer it is. In sum, the more sweet foods appear in the dream, the greater the happiness of the one who dreams.

The path the disciple took to reach his home in the dream represents his journey on the spiritual path. The chocolate that fell during this journey symbolizes the many difficulties this disciple has faced as a *Karkarī* from Algeria. Despite everything, he held on and remained on the path. Most disciples would have abandoned the path in the face of the trials this disciple endured. The fact that he reached the end of the journey indicates that this disciple will be among those whom Allah ﷻ will reward generously. The greatest *rizq* that Allah ﷻ can give him is a healthy connection between him and his family. Now, it is his responsibility to guide them toward the Light. This kind of *da'wa* is among the blessed gateways that lead disciples to righteous deeds.

*

Everything That Comes from the Sea Is Pure

A woman saw in a dream a man named Riḍwān giving her fish.

Everything that comes from the sea is pure (*ṭahūr*) and lawful (*ḥalāl*), whether it be fish, coral, or pearls. Seeing this in a dream is good news. The more beautiful, large, and high-quality the fish, the greater the *rizq* the disciple will receive. Conversely, smaller, lower-quality, or sick fish signify a weaker *rizq*.

If in the dream the disciple sees someone giving him a large quantity of fish without any effort on his part, it means his *rizq* will come to him with ease. Conversely, if he sees himself fishing and exerting a lot of effort to catch the fish, it means he will have to work hard to obtain his *rizq*.

In the dream, the man is named Riḍwān, which means "satisfaction".

In the dream, this man is dressed according to the sunna: he wears white clothing and has a beard. This indicates that she shall marry a good man, who follows the sunna of the Prophet ﷺ.

*

Completing the Manifestation of an Incomplete Name Through *Dhikr* and Following the *Sunna*

Another disciple saw the name of the Prophet ﷺ in a vision, but without the dāl (د). She saw the Arabic letters of Muḥammad (م ح م) and of Aḥmad (م ح أ), missing the dāl in both.

It has been reported in several hadiths that the Prophet ﷺ explained that the best of names are those that contain the term ʿabd, such as ʿAbd Allāh and ʿAbd al-Raḥmān, as well as names that include al-ḥamd, like Muḥammad, Ḥamdi, and Maḥmūd. In this dream, the disciple saw one of the best names, but without the Arabic letter dāl.

The dāl refers to the concept of dawām (continuity).

To understand the name Muḥammad ﷺ, one must know that the mīm of this name is annihilated in the hāʾ of the name "Allāh". For this annihilation to be perpetual, the dāl of continuity must be present. In this vision, the sister must strive to complete the name by adding the dāl through more dhikr.

In general, when the disciple sees an incomplete name or verse in a vision, he must make more *dhikr* to complete it.

Furthermore, in Islam, the name of the Prophet Muḥammad ﷺ symbolizes the sunna. The disciple's vision of his incomplete name suggests that she is lacking in her adherence to the sunna. There are aspects of the sunna that she is not fully practicing, but she should. If we interpret her vision through the four luminous exemplifications, it is as if she has gathered the niche, the crystal, and the Lamp without yet bringing them together in the Radiant Star. This disciple must strive to reach the Radiant Star and anchor herself within it.

*

Love in *al-Qabḍ*

This same disciple says she witnesses a moving star. She sometimes feels a contraction in her chest during dhikr and wonders if this contraction comes from her darkened nafs or from the name of Allah ﷻ al-Qābiḍ (the Contractor).

All *qabḍ* comes from the *nafs*. The one who enters the tariqa and dislikes being alone and isolated, preferring the company of others, will be more prone to *qabḍ*. The one who seeks Allah ﷻ must isolate himself to be in spiritual seclusion (*khulwa*) with Him ﷻ. The one who does not love seclusion does not love being with Allah ﷻ and is far from Him ﷻ.

Contraction primarily stems from the love of the *dunyā*. The one who becomes poor during his journey must say *al-ḥamdu lillāh*, for Allah ﷻ has protected him from the *fitna* of wealth. He can then devote himself exclusively to Allah ﷻ.

The people of Allah report that the one who loves Allah will face the trial of poverty, while the one who loves the Prophet ﷺ will face the trial of illness, and the one who loves his family will face the trial of enemies.

The one who loves Allah ﷻ loves to be in *khulwa* with Him ﷻ. When he is in *khulwa*, he prays to Allah ﷻ and hopes that no one disturbs or interrupts this moment of intimacy with his Lord ﷻ. The one who is truly present with Allah ﷻ does not boast about how much he prays or fasts. This is not love. The one who loves Allah ﷻ naturally loves prayer and takes his time in performing it. He savors every moment of his prayer with serenity, carrying out each movement and recitation with deliberation. When in prostration, he lingers in that state, prolonging the moment of closeness to his Lord.

*

How to Love Seclusion

One should practice secluding oneself in a quiet place to perform *dhikr*. To avoid fatigue and boredom, it's important to change the type of worship when the *nafs* begins to tire and craves something different. Instead of leaving the place, shift to another form of worship, such as transitioning from prayer to reciting the Qur'ān. If the *nafs* continues to desire something else afterward, remain in the same place and continue performing *dhikr*.

In this way, you will add depth and variety to your journey on the paths of *īmān*. This is how you will cultivate a love for isolation and the company of Allah ﷻ.

In the past, the people of Allah ﷻ would go on pilgrimages alone and avoid the markets. They wished to preserve their relationship with Allah ﷻ and protect it from being diminished by worldly interactions. Thus, they would venture alone into the *mulk* of Allah (the physical world) to invoke Him after their *khulwa*.

*

When Allah Responds to Our Prayers

During the du'ā' of Friday prayer, a disciple saw the Lamp expand until it filled the heavens and the earth. He also asked Sidi Shaykh to pray for his healing from illness.

It should not be said that the Lamp in your heart filled the heavens and the earth, but rather that it filled the horizons of your heart. Whoever sees the Lamp in this way should offer the prayers they desire, and Allah ﷻ will answer them.

*

The Love of the Righteous Leads to the *Walī*

A disciple tells us she had two interconnected dreams. The first dream occurred fifteen years ago. She saw herself sitting in the maqām (tomb) of a walī. Then she saw someone above this maqām pour a bottle of rose water, and the disciple extended her hands to catch some of this water. When the water reached her hands, it gushed forth explosively. The second dream occurred after she took the hand with Sidi Shaykh. In this dream, Sidi Shaykh was praying and reading the Qur'ān in the same maqām she saw in the first dream.

Water represents life and purification. The water she discovered in the *maqām* is what revived her and brought her to the ultimate purification of her *nafs*. Through this water, she returned to her Lord ﷻ. The fact that she had this dream fifteen years ago indicates that the love of the righteous (*ṣāliḥīn*) led her to the Shaykh. The *awliyā'* (sg. *walī*) act as a talisman (*ṭalsam*) that guides people back to Allah. They should not be reduced to their physical appearance. All *awliyā'* carry *wilāya* (sainthood), just as all Prophets carry Prophethood (*nubuwwa*). The only difference is that al-Muṣṭafā ﷺ united them all and sealed Prophethood and the Message.

Wilāya, however, continues through the *'itra*, as the Prophet ﷺ indicated. The People of his Family will accompany us until we reach the basin facing the gate of Paradise.

*

Everything Begins with a Flash

A disciple saw a Flash of Light in a vision. This Flash then became a Radiant Star, which she says she sometimes sees even with her eyes open. She also perceives the Blessed Tree in Light, and when she eats or drinks, she feels that it is not her hand moving but that of her Lord ﷻ. She believes that existence prostrates before her.

When the Flash illuminates the heart, the disciple inherits the Cloud of the Prophet ﷺ. Beneath the shade of this Cloud sat the Beloved ﷺ when he was a child. When this Cloud appears in the heart, it brings rain, and the Blessed Tree—the Olive Tree that transcends all directions—will be planted there. The water that falls from this Cloud purifies the heart.

*

Everything Prostrates

The disciple then asks, "How can I avoid self-satisfaction and arrogance?"

Always remember that some disciples never cease witnessing the resplendent Star. These disciples are constantly in its company and are far better than you. Also, if you feel that your hand is the hand of Allah ﷻ know that there are disciples who have become so absorbed in their Lord ﷻ that they no longer feel their own existence. Return to Allah ﷻ and everything will return to you.

Understand that everything prostrates before you—not out of worship, but because Allah ﷻ has granted humanity the mandate of *khilāfa* (Vicegerency). Things love you only because of your love for Allah ﷻ. Recognize that everything must prostrate, each in its own degree. You too will prostrate. The human body prostrates here on earth, but the spirit prostrates in one of the seven heavens or at the Lote Tree of the Farthest Boundary (*muntahā*).

The goal is to move toward Allah ﷻ and never return to the world of phantoms, the world of nonexistence. To avoid arrogance, remember that some disciples dive into the Shaykh, reaching the part of his being they seek in order to draw knowledge from it.

Session XIV
August 18, 2021

*

The Use of Charity and *Zakāt* Funds in the *Zāwiya*

The following are the eight points mentioned in one of Sidi Shaykh's sessions regarding the sources of expenditure in the *Zāwiya*, whether from *zakāt*, *ṣadaqa*, or other sources. These points are intended to clarify any confusion some disciples may have on this matter.

1.

The prohibition of consuming *ṣadaqa* and *zakāt* by the Shaykh and his family does not imply a prohibition for the disciples present in the *Zāwiya*. On the contrary, one of the most important sources of expenditure in the *sharīʿa* to fulfill the needs of the disciples journeying in the path of self-purification, as well as those of the *Zāwiya*, comes from charity and *zakāt*. This is clearly illustrated in the story of the Prophet ﷺ with Sayyidunā Salmān al-Fārisī ؓ. When Salmān decided to give charity, the Prophet ﷺ distributed it among his Companions and did not forbid them from consuming it, though he refrained

235

from it himself. This demonstrates that any money given for the repair or construction of the *Zāwiya* or for the expenses of the disciples is permissible. *Zakāt* and charity constitute the majority of the *Zāwiya*'s funding, and those who refrain from contributing, for whatever reason, have no understanding of how the *Zāwiya* operates.

2.

In the path, the miser (*al-bakhīl*) will never reach the divine assembly (*ḥaḍra*) and will be deprived of it. *Al-Karīm* (the Generous) is indeed one of the Most Beautiful Names of Allah ﷻ. The Almighty ﷻ has said in His blessed Book in *Sūra* al-Tawba: **"Indeed, Allah has purchased from the believers their lives and their wealth, in exchange for Paradise."** The Arabic word for wealth is *māl*, derived from *mayalān*, which means inclination or attraction. The first level of this inclination is the love of wealth and private property. Other inclinations follow, such as custom, differences in jurisprudential understanding, and doctrinal issues. Whoever seeks the favor of his Lord would sell his wealth and/or property, and thus all inclinations. Sayyidunā Mūsā ﷺ sold his inclination to Sayyidunā al-Khiḍr ﷺ by accepting, albeit reluctantly, the destruction of the ship and the killing of the young boy. Sayyidunā Mūsā ﷺ made this sacrifice to attain the highest goal: the knowledge of the Almighty ﷻ.

Sidi Shaykh tells us the story of a *walī* who was particularly wealthy to illustrate what it means to sell one's inclinations. The Creator had enriched him with His grace. Yet, when a disciple came to him, he would ask for gifts and money. One day, a disciple asked him why he required gifts when Allah ﷻ had granted him sufficient wealth. He replied: "If we, the *awliyā*, spend from the most precious thing we possess, which is the knowledge of the Creator, then the disciple should be obliged to spend from the most precious thing to him. And there is nothing more precious to the disciple than the *dunyā*. Therefore, he must spend from it until he obtains the most precious thing we possess, which is *ma'rifa*."

3.

Zakāt is one of the pillars of Islam. Whoever purifies his wealth is indeed purifying himself and his belongings from filth. There are numerous examples from the stories of the companions on spending wealth for the love of Allah ﷻ and His Prophet ﷺ. Among the most famous is Sayyidunā Abū Bakr ﷺ who, when the Prophet ﷺ requested aid to fill the state treasury, brought all he possessed and placed it in the honorable hands of the Messenger ﷺ. When the Prophet ﷺ asked what he had left for his children, he replied, "Allah and His Messenger." Upon returning home, Sayyidunā Abū Bakr ﷺ found that Allah ﷻ had provided for him. Know that your home, before being a roof and walls, is your heart, where the Creator has placed His secrets. As for Sayyidunā 'Umar ﷺ, he did not completely empty his heart of his wealth and children. These inclinations remained in him, even though he presented half of his wealth to the beloved Prophet ﷺ. Half of his heart remained inclined toward his family and wealth. The two examples are not equal.

4.

The wayfarer should know that the money taken by al-Muṣṭafā ﷺ from the Companions in terms of charity and *zakāt* was used to build the Islamic state by developing lands, equipping the armies of Islam, and financing other public works. These expenditures were not solely for the poor and needy; in fact, that category of expenditure was a small part of a comprehensive list that contributed to the establishment of religion and the Islamic state. Therefore, it is truly strange that a disciple who has spent a year, a month, or even a week in this blessed place, the *Zāwiya*, who has eaten its food, slept under its blankets, and purified himself with its water, would turn away when it comes to giving his *zakāt* or *ṣadaqa* to the house of knowledge and the source of the Light of the Prophet ﷺ. What is even more perplexing is when he chooses to spend this money elsewhere, whether on building mosques or helping common Muslims. We do not deny that he will be rewarded by Allah ﷻ—this is indisputable—but in terms of knowledge and the path to the *ḥaḍra* of the Creator, he will not gain any share. In *Sūra* al-Tawba, verse 103, the Almighty ﷻ says to the Prophet ﷺ: **"Take, [O Muḥammad], from their wealth a charity by which you purify them and cause them to increase, and invoke [Allah's blessings] upon them. Indeed, your invocations are reasSūrance for them. And Allah is Hearing and Knowing."** The one purified and blessed by the Prophet ﷺ, through his heir, who is refined and connected to the *ḥaḍra*, and who provides a dwelling in that *ḥaḍra*, cannot be compared to one who merely receives a reward for a good deed. The one connected to the Prophet ﷺ gains far more, and this is beyond doubt.

5.

It is essential to know that the Shaykh and his family do not take even a penny from this money. However, the Shaykh accepts gifts and support from his two brothers—may Allah be pleased with them. He earns money from *ruqya*, which is Sidi Shaykh's profession. The public should know that if the *walī* wanted to become wealthy, it would be the easiest thing for him. He prefers, however, to sit with his disciples, educate them, accompany them in their journey toward Allah ﷻ, and help them solve their daily problems rather than devote himself to his profession. Indeed, the Shaykh's sessions with his disciples are more valuable than the gold of the world.

6.

The *walī* is the only servant of Allah ﷻ for whom He will hold all the descendants of Ādam ﷺ accountable on the Day of Judgment. Imam Muslim ﷺ reports in his *Ṣaḥīḥ* that the Prophet ﷺ said: "Allah will say on the Day of Resurrection: 'O son of Ādam, I was sick, and you did not visit Me!' The man will reply: 'Lord, how could I visit You when You are the Lord of the worlds?' Allah will say: 'Did you not know that My servant, so-and-so, was sick, and you did not visit him? Had you visited him, you would have found Me with him. O son of Ādam, I asked you for food, and you did not feed Me!' The man will reply: 'Lord, how could I feed You when You are the Lord of the worlds?' Allah will say: 'Did you not know that so-and-so asked you for food, and you did not feed him? Had you fed him, you would have found the reward for your action with Me. O son of Ādam, I asked you for a drink, and you did not give Me drink!' The man will reply: 'Lord, how could I give You drink when You are the Lord of the worlds?' Allah will say: 'So-and-so asked you for a drink, and you refused to give him. Did you not know that had you given him drink, you would have found the reward for your action with Me?'"

In this hadith, the address is directed to all of humanity, not just the believers who have taken *bay'a*. This servant mentioned in the hadith is none other than God's vicegerent (*al-khalīfa*) because he is the only one who can lead you to Allah ﷻ. All humanity is accounted for when he requests something.

As for the *bay'a*, it concerns only the group of believers (*mu'minīn*), not all Muslims, as referenced in the verse of the *walī*. Therefore, if the *walī* requests money, the believer should give it with full understanding, knowing that this act is more valuable than spending money elsewhere. The believer must recognize that, through these expenditures under the *walī's* guidance, his heart will be illuminated by the Light of the four luminous exemplifications, which Allah ﷻ has placed in his hands. And there is nothing more valuable than this Light, the Elixir of life. If one glance at the face of the *walī* is worth more than seventy years of worship, how much greater is the value of spending even one dirham in his presence? The wise understand that this surpasses even seventy years of spending outside the circle of the *ḥaḍra*.

7.

The *walī* has granted permission for elevation to those who are not distracted by trade or sale and who are in continuous *dhikr* of Allah ﷻ. Through this permission (*idhn*), Allah has enriched them with His generosity and blessed their sustenance (*rizq*). They have thus obtained the best of this world and the hereafter. They, too, spend in the path of Allah ﷻ to see their trade blessed and their journey shortened. They are obliged to pass through the *wilāya*, the only door that leads them to Allah, in terms of expenditures.

8.

There are degrees of spending in the path of the Prophet ﷺ. The one who spends only *zakāt* has a share in the knowledge of certainty (*'ilm al-yaqīn*). Such a person does not surpass the degree of Islam. The one who spends a fifth of his wealth on the *wilāya* is at the level of the essence of certainty (*'ayn al-yaqīn*) or the station of faith (*īmān*). However, the one who has given all his wealth to the Real has reached the station of the core of certainty (*ḥaqq al-yaqīn*) or the station of *iḥsān*.

And let the disciple know that the path to the Real passes through the elite of the Family of the Prophet ﷺ. Finally, do you, disciples, think that the Companions of the Messenger of Allah ﷺ gave all their wealth to the Prophet ﷺ and said: "O Messenger of Allah, what will you give us from your wealth?" They believed that their wealth and their very selves belonged to the Prophet ﷺ who is the true guardian of their blessings, and they renounced their inclinations, thoughts, and illusions concerning any material possessions.

Printed and bound
in the United States of America